GUERNICA
THE MAKING OF A PAINTING

© SILEX®: 1983
S.P.A.D.E.M.-S.G.A.E.: 1983
I.S.B.N.: 84-85041-76-3
Copyright: M. 361-1983
Layout: J. M. Domínguez
Printed in Spain by: ASTYGI. Coslada (Madrid)
(Printed in Spain)
Translated by:
Josefine Bregazzi

GUERNICA
THE MAKING OF A PAINTING

Joaquín de la Puente

CONTENTS

BY WAY OF PREAMBLE

One may assume that the dates of the 24th and 25th of October 1981 will be remembered as a doubly remarkable joint occasion within the context of Spanish artistic and museum culture of the twentieth century. For on these two days the two successive inaugurations —both the public and the official— of **Guernica** were held, as likewise the commemoration of the painter's first centenary of birth. The painter, of course, was the universal Malagan, Pablo Ruiz Picasso. **Guernica** has for many years been the most resounding pictorial voice of that young but exemplary museum, the Museum of Modern Art in New York, in which Picasso was wise enough to place it in safekeeping from Tyrians and Trojans, whilst its permanent destination was awaited. The story of this will be told in the following pages.

After its arrival in Spain, **Guernica** and a considerable number of others of the painter's works once more became the property of the Prado Museum (created in 1819) on that memorable day in October 1981. Moreover, the Museum was physically enlarged in 1971, by using the Casón del Buen Retiro, as though someone could then foresee that ten years later the most famous painting of the most renowned painter of our century was to be exhibited there. It was as though both chance and need, which it is said are the driving forces of all that exists, had worked together by themselves and in good time in order to offer an immediately worthy and idoneous resting-place to a work which the painter had categorically stated to be destined for the Prado Museum. For one might even suppose that no other Spanish museum could be a better or more symbolic precinct than the Casón for the homage which *Guernica* deserved and which we wished to render it.

In the first place, the Casón is, I repeat since 1971, an unquestionable part of our greatest Museum. In the second place, on account of the heightened relief which the mere fact of its physical separation from the larger main building lends whatever is exhibited there, thus highlighting it from the huge, overwhelming muddle of Velázquez's, Goya's, Titian's and other myriad marvels which sieze one in the original Prado Building. Thirdly, we chose it because it is literally the type of regal environment of what was originally a ballroom, in which **Guernica** is exhibited, it was not long before it was used for the distinguished and courtly receptions offered to ambassadors, which lent it a noble quality that few other buildings possess —noble enough, in fact, to house Picasso and his work, and with a highly suggestive history, the outline of which must be given here, albeit as briefly as possible.

The Casón is one of the two remains of the Buen Retiro Palace, which was built in the 17th century by Philip IV. The other of these two remains is the nearby Army Museum which still preserves the Kingdoms Room for which Velázquez painted his famous *Lanzas*. The Casón is situated where previously, outside the old city walls, and later of the court of Madrid, the Catholic Monarchs had founded the Royal Monastery of St. Jerome, with a church that, although much restored, is still preserverd, a large orchard and the so-called «St.

14

Jerome Room» for the withdrawal, devotions, leisure and rest of the Spanish sovereigns. Philip II enlarged it, with the whim that some of its nooks and crannies should be given a certain British air, having seen parks and gardens in England upon the occasion of his marriage to Mary Tudor.

It seems that the actual instigator of the idea of the Buen Retiro Palace was the Count of Olivares. Perhaps it was built because the Madrid palace was not in fact very healthy, as was alleged among other things in the public justification of the works. Perhaps also, it was due to the fact that the monarchs were themselves convinced that the cost of such a huge architectonic undertaking would compensate for the «heavy expenses and many inconveniences» caused by their summer trips to the then royal sites of Aranjuez, El Escorial and El Pardo.

In 1630 or 1631, Alonso Carbonel —or Carbonell— began his work. He showed himself to be a deft hand at quick work. Those parts of the building which were designed to be the main ones were inaugurated in 1632. In 1637 Carbonell was commissioned to build the ballroom, the Casón, and probably finished it the following year. It appears in 1656 parallel to the Salón de Comedias or Coliseum, on Pedro Texeira's map of Madrid. We know from a certain royal warrant how pleased Philip IV was with the finished work of the palace built for him. In it, Velázquez and a number of other artists were given work, the great Spanish drama of the 17th century was performed in it and fastuous banquets were held there. It also served as a cover for political intrigue and business and, of course, for the religious retreats which the devoutly Catholic members of the House of Austria never failed to practise.

It is said that Charles II, the son and heir of Philip IV, did not at first display much enthusiasm for the Buen Retiro Palace. However he was eventually to take an interest in it, it being he himself who decided that the Casón should be granted high rank by converting it into the Ambassadors' Room. In the same way, it was Charles II himself who in 1694 or 1695 commissioned the Spanish-Neopolitan, Lucas Jordán or Lucca Giordano, with its fastuous decoration after making him paint the El Escorial fresco and the vestry of Toledo Cathedral. All that is left of Jordán's work in the Casón is the fresco on its great dome. In this fresco, he portrayed the «Origin and Triumph in Spain of the Order of the Toison d'Or», founded in 1429 by Philip the Good, Duke of Burgundy and Brabant and confirmed in 1433 by Pope Eugene IV, to be then passed on to the Spanish crown through the Emperor Charles V, the Spanish crown still holding the dignity of grand master of the order. Of those works painted by Jordan which are now missing, one should mention «The Efforts and Prowesses of Hercules» which was painted on the lower cornice of the dome, other paintings on the Granada War in the days of the Catholic Monarchs, an allegory of the Sun led by Aurora and the Four Corners of the World, these latter works distributed in the two antechambers of the building. Luckily, a great deal of these are recorded for us in excellent engravings of the 18th century.

When the old Madrid Palace was burnt down in 1734, Philip V, the first of our Bourbon kings, had no other alternative but to move to the Buen

Retiro Palace. This latter thus became the main Seat of a monarchy which still possessed an immense part of the earth. It was moreover to remain an imperial palace until the present one was made inhabitable in the reign of Charles III, which Philip V, faithful to the spirit of his ancestors of the House of Austria, had built on the same site on which the burned-down Palace had stood which had cost Philip II so much effort and in which Philip IV had stored so much artistic wealth. A large part of this was saved from the flames by the people of Madrid and forms the basic funds of the Prado Museum.

The Casón was meant to be the place in which to welcome Napoleón in April 1808, unawares that the War of Independence was only a step away, as likewise other nearby outbuildings of the palace. On the 2nd of May 1808, however, the popular uprising against the French broke out and the French at once turned the Buen Retiro Palace into barracks, thus causing damages for this reason alone and even more on the 12th of August 1812, when our allies, the English, had to take the building by assault. Once the war was over, there was information around 1815 in the sense that the Casón was precisely one of the buildings which had least suffered from the eight years of the ferocious war. The fact is that Ferdinand VII took pains to repair both large and small damages suffered by the palace as a whole.

Upon the death of Ferdinand VII, his widow, the Queen-Regent, María Cristina of Bourbon, established the «Estamento de Próceres» or Senate in the Casón in 1834, after somewhat unfortunate alterations. Once the Senate had occupied the

Seat it still holds in Madrid, the Casón between 1841 and 1854 housed the Topographic Cabinet or Museum created by Charles IV, which had been seriously damaged by the French and later rebuilt and re-installed by Ferdinand VII in the Kingdoms Room, mentioned at the beginning as the present Army Museum.

For several years the Casón became the riding-school and gymnasium of Alfonso XII when he was Prince of Asturias. After the 1868 Revolution, the wealth of the Crown passed over to the national patrimony. The Government and the Madrid City Council together plotted to begin the destruction of the Buen Retiro Palace, and were one and the other willing to allow speculation of the site and create a residential area which still stands today. Only the Army Museum and the Casón were saved from demolition. In this latter, Amadeus I of Savoy inaugurated an Artistic and Industrial Exhibition in 1871 which, curiously, we may perhaps consider to be somewhat unexpected as a modest forerunner to the great Exhibition, likewise devoted to Art and Industry, which in Paris in 1938 housed Picasso's *Guernica*.

The politician Antonio Cánovas del Castillo created the Museum of Artistic Reproductions in 1878. This was an exemplary institution in which Picasso drew at least during the first of his stays in Madrid, and which was soon to become known by the nick—name of the building in which it was housed: the Casón. Cánovas added the two side-wings, those of the rooms in which the works accompanying **Guernica** are now exhibited. In 1960, with unheard—of speed and unconceivable brutality, the Museum of Artistic Reproductions

18

was dismantled, with the consequent irreplaceable loss of many of its valuable possessions. This outrage is not, moreover, justified by the fact that it was committed to hold the Velázquez exhibition in the Casón and that it was in future to serve as exhibition rooms for the General Direction of Fine Arts' highly important exhibitions. It was later installed on the top floor of the Central Restoration Institute. In 1971, the Commissariat for Artistic Patrimony, which was later to become the general Sub-Direction of same, was installed on the same floor. Then, on this same noble floor, the Section of 19th Century Art of the Prado Museum was opened to the public, thus removing from the Spanish Museum of Contemporary Art works which some voluble legislator had considered to be indispensable to it upon its creation in 1968.

Exactly 10 years later, in 1981, straight after numerous new internal alterations and the creation of the General Sub-Direction of Artistic Patrimony, the Casón displayed a renewed and enlarged Section of 19th Century Art and the world-famous **Guernica** and Picasso legacy.

This is more or less a quick synthesis of what I believe should be said about the Casón, before we go on to discuss what really matters to us here: a probing of our vision and opinion of Picasso's **Guernica** within its historical context and dense creative environment. We should warn the reader who is in a hurry to turn to this that he should perhaps not stop over the detailed biography of the painter which comes at the beginning and which was necessary for, as one's reading progresses and on other occassions, one finds how useful it is to have the biography to hand.

Naturally, much of what I have written in this, what I intend to be dense, work, coincides with others' points of view. This is not so much on account of the fact that I was aware of these views previously as because I personally reached the same or similar conclusions through direct observation of the works discussed. I always follow this method which tautens both my reflexive capacity and my vision... In the present case, this method has brought me a new experience with regard to **Guernica** and its environment and what I have so far been able to read in it. This new experience, together with the rest, which I have been largely advocating in classes and talks for years is what I decided to set forth in this condensed book of mine. It was written with ideas which border on the obsessive with respect to being precise for I will not steal any further time than necessary from readers who are so short of time and have many other types of printed matter to take in and innumerable works of art to contemplate at leisure. For it is said that an image is worth a thousand words and that the reader should also be allowed a margin of time for observation, so that he does not fall into the usual trap of believing that he has really looked properly at all that he «sees» on the sole bias of the thousand and one interpretations let loose all over. That these latter are good insofar as they are such is true, but they should not interfere with one's own perception or the unhurried individual savouring of the great creations of the spirit —**Guernica,** for example— which are intended to be food for the eyes, and for the oft despised sensorial and visual intelligence.

PICASSO, STEP BY STEP: 1881-1973

As is stated above, this summarised biography may be of greater use if read after the following texts which refer directly to Picasso's works exhibited in the Casón, for the texts make it necessary.

From birth to the end of the «Pink Period» (1881-1906)

Picasso was born in the Plaza de la Merced in Málaga, on the 25th October, **1881.** According to the devout Spanish custom of the time, he was baptised and endowed with a good measure of the Christian Sanctoral calendar: Pablo, Diego, José, Francisco de paula, Juan Nepomuceno, María de los Remedios, Crispín and Crispiniano de la Santísima Trinidad[1]. The son of a humble drawing master at the San Telmo School of Arts and Crafts in Málaga and keeper of the city museum, José Ruiz Blasco (1838-1903) and his wife María Picasso López (1855-1939), he was the eldest of their offspring. His sisters Lola and Conchita were born in 1884 and 1887 and died in 1958 and 1895 respectively. When he was just under ten, he was taken to Corunna, where José Ruiz Blasco was to

---

[1] These two latter were the saints of the day. «Cipriano» was doubtless written on the baptism certificate in error, whilst María de los Remedios was omitted at the Registry Office. The remaining names were those of so many other saints whose names had been given to members of his family and Pablo was the name of one of his uncles, a canon who, until his death, was a staunch supporter of his brother, José Ruiz Blasco, Picasso's father.

work as drawing master in a secondary school. The boy, who was unusually precocious, drew and painted constantly. Between **1891** and **1894,** he thought out, illustrated and wrote two small magazines for himself, his friends and family: «La Coruña» and «Azul y Blanco». In April of **1895,** José Ruiz Blasco changed his job in Corunna for another in Barcelona as master of figure drawing at the School of Fine Arts of La Lonja. To this end, after a trip to Madrid which enabled Pablo to see the wonders of the Prado Museum for the first time, and after a summer holiday in Malaga, the whole family moved to Barcelona in the month of September. Picasso was then about a month under the age of fourteen. During the same month of September 1895, when he arrived in Barcelona, he passed the entrance exam to the Escuela Superior de Bellas Artes de San Jorge, or La Lonja School of Fine Arts. His father supplied him with and paid for personal study in **1896.** During the same years, he sent *The First Communion* to the Barcelona Municipal Exhibition. Stating himself to be a pupil of Antonio Muñoz Degrain in the catalogue, he won an honorific mention in the National Fine Arts Exhibition in Madrid in 1897 and the gold medal in the provincial one in Malaga with his *Science and Charity*. On account of his youth, his pictorial vision at this time displayed the still prevailing nineteenth-century realism. His summers in Malaga kept alive his deep-rooted and incorruptible Andalusian spirit. In Madrid, also in **1897,** he entered the San Fernando School of Fine Arts, drew in the Casón —the Museum of Artistic Reproductions— and was a regular visitor to the Prado. In June of **1898,** a simple case of scarlet

fever put an end to his stay in Madrid and forced him to return to his family in Barcelona to recover. Together with his friend, Manuel Pallarés, he came to know Horta de Ebro (Tarragona), a town which as from 1919 was given the name of Horta de San Juan and which made a profound impression on him: «All that I know, I learned in Horta de Ebro», he said later; this is where he is said to have painted *Aragonese Customs,* a work which he is also said to have won the third medal in the National Exhibition of the same year (1898) with, although it is not known that he did not compete sufficently to get this award; it is certain that this work is confused with a *Patio of a House in Aragón* which won an honorific mention in the National Exhibition of **1899.** Certain problems with his family led him to leave home to lodge in his artist friends' studios and even in houses of «bad fame». He thus met the poet Jaime Sabartés years later and who until his death in 1968 was his secretary. He moved with ease within the rich cultural ethos of the modernist beer-house «Els Quatre Gats» and atten-ded the Sunday coterie of Carlos Casagemas and the gatherings of Juan Vidal Ventosa. He gradually abandoned nineteenth-century realism with its direct vision. In **1900,** he lived in Casagemas' studio and exhibited in «Els Quatre Gats» with a series of portrait drawings which displayed both his skill and a hint of Ramón Casas' influence on him. He began to publish illustrations in «Joventut». Shortly after his nineteenth birthday —at the end of October 1900— he made his first trip to Paris together with Casagemas and Manuel Pallarés and stayed with Isidro Nonell. Toulouse-Lautrec's work both impressed and affected him. He returned to

Barcelona in December and went directly to Malaga with a view to finding some amusement for the melancholic Casagemas. In January 1901 he went to Madrid. Casagemas committed suicide in Paris on February 17th, as his love for Germaine Pichot was not returned. The loss of his friend profoundly affected Picasso. He took part in the National Exhibition of Fine Arts with *A Figure,* the work we know today as *Woman in Blue,* which was not withdrwan from the Exhibition and therefore became the property of the National Museum of Modern Art. It is at present in the Spanish Museum of Contemporary Art. There is no doubt that, although he knew Barcelona well and had tasted the brilliance of Paris, he now tried to continue his career in Madrid. In March he launched the first number of «Arte Joven» together with Francisco de Asís Soler. They did not manage to publish more than five numbers and he returned to Barcelona around the middle of May. From June to July and together with Ramón Casas, he carried out an exhibition of mainly Parisian pastel drawings in the Parés gallery. In June he made his second trip to Paris, encouraged by a contract —his whole output for a hundred and fifty Francs a month— offered to him by Pedro Manyac —or Mañach— a Catalan art dealer. From the 25th June to the 14th July of the same year (1901) he exhibited in the Vollard Gallery with Francisco Iturrino. He met Max Jacob at the exhibition. Jaime Sabartés came to stay with him. He took parte in the Escuelas Albia exhibition in Bilbao and in October exhibited five works in a collective at the Witcomb Gallery in Buenos Aires. In the autumn, he launched what was to become known as his

28

blue period once and for all. He travelled to Barcelona in January **1902,** having broken his contract with Manyac, the art dealer. He lived with his family and met and became acquainted with Eugenio d'Ors. From the 1st to the 15th April, he exhibited in Paris at the Berthe Weill Gallery together with Louis Bernard Lemaire. From the 2nd to the 15th June, he participated in a collective at the same gallery. In October he undertook his third raid on Paris and finished by sharing his own poverty with that of Max Jacob. From the 15th November to the 15th December, he exhibited in the Berthe Weill Gallery with Giriaud, Launay and Pichot. The cold and harsh Bohemian life led him once more to Barcelona with his family at the beginning of 1903, where he began the preparatory sketches for the great painting *Life*. He began to achieve a certain name for himself. In 1904 he managed to get his own studio and left his family. In April, he once more travelled to Paris, where he lived with the so-called and later famous «Bateau-Lavoir» —in a hut in the Rue Ravignan in Montmartre— where Paco Durrio, Max Jacob, Van Dongen, André Salmón also lived and where he was to meet the beautiful Fernande Olivier with whom he was to live until 1912. The near—by Medrano circus was a source of inspiration for some of his works. From the 24th October to the 20th November he exhibited in the Berthe Weill Gallery with Charbonnier, Clary-Baroux, Dufy, Giriaud, Picabia and Thiesson. Eugenio d'Ors prophesied a great future for him in the Barcelona magazine «El poble català». His *blue period* ends here. In 1906, his *pink period* began. He met the wealthy Americans Leo and Gertrude Stein and

Caricature of a violinist

Family of acrobats

Guillaume Apollinaire. From the 25th February to the 6th March, he exhibited with Trachsel and Gérardin in the Serrurier Gallery. In the summer he travelled to Holland invited by the writer Schilperoot. At the end of April 1906 he went to Barcelona with his friend Fernande Olivier. He spent a large part of the spring and summer with her at Gósol (Lérida). He carried out important work in drawing and gouache painting, although not in oils. They were obliged to leave for Paris once more on account of an outbreak of typhoid fever. At the end of 1906, he finished with his *pink period* and had already achieved a not unestimable name for himself in Paris. Thus a whole vast cycle came to its close which had gone from his early beginnings to the very threshold of what was to be for him Cubism. He had gone through an initial stage of nineteenth-century vision, the influence of Barcelona modernism, the impact of El Greco, the influence of Toulouse-Lautrec and the outburst of his own decisive peronality in his *blue* and pink periods. He had turned out a vast production with such notable works as *The Embrace, Life, The Girl with the Crow, The Harlequin's Family, Family of Acrobats with Monkey, Seated Harlequin, Portrait of Mrs. Canals, Nude Girl with Horse* and so forth, a rich, diverse and unmistakably Picassian output, which in the *blue period* was lyrical and even sentimental and in the *pink period* became concerned with grace and jovial luminosity. He also displayed a fertile self-confidence which was never to leave him until his death.

From Cubism to the Outbreak of Surrealism (1907-1925)

From **1906,** in which his *pink period* came to an end, Picasso was in the process of giving bith to a most spectacular artistic and intellectual event. Cézanne, Iberian art exhibited in the Louvre in 1906, a certain statuary monumentality and the creations of primitive nations —black sculpture mainly— germinated in his mind and prepared it for the creation of the perhaps most innovating of

20th century contemporary art aesthetics, Cubism. Picasso's pro-Cubism of 1906 was to be thus and was to absorb all his plastic and artistically re-volutionary power, later affecting Braque and a little later other painter friends of his. His summer in Gósol, Spain (Lérida) near the French frontier was decisive. Under the impact caused by the African works in the Trocadero Museum —the Museum of Man— his *black period* began in **1907**. In his studio in Bateau Lavoir, Montmartre, he studied human form feverishly in search of a new structural syntax which was to be synthetic and schematic as opposed to any imitative vision of the natural; it was even to be idealizing. He then began the now mythical *Demoiselles d'Avignon* —the «young ladies» of a brothel in d'Avinyó Street in Barcelona— who, at first, could hardly be under-stood by his more daring friends of the Parisian avant-garde: Matisse, Derain, Vollard.. Certain German friends such as Uhde and Kahnweiler did understand him, however. Fernande Olivier in «Picasso and his friends» mentions how Braque argued with all the passion an artist is capable of against what Picasso the portraying in this and in other canvasses. However, in order to clarify and to a certain extent, to corroborate such a plastic intuition, the exhibition of fifty-six of Cézanne's works was held in the Autumn Salon and his principle that nature should be re-shaped in the geometricizing light of the cylinder, the sphere and the cone, was made known in print. This occurred after the other groups of works by Cézanne which the Salon had been exhibiting in Paris since 1904. (*Les Demoiselles d'Avignon* was kept rolled up in Picasso's studio until 1920 and was printed in the

Self-portrait

«Révolution Surréaliste» of 1925, exhibited in the
Petit Palais in 1937 and inmediately acquired by
the New York Museum of Modern Art, with which
it achieved the universal artistic prestige it now

possesses.) In **1908** Picasso continued unswervingly in his aims. Whilst Braque, inadvertently captivated, as Fernande Olivier points out, by Picasso's new path, exhibited in the Autumn Salon works which were to give rise to a certain irony on the part of Matisse and, following this, to the fact the critic Louis Vauxcelles should speak of «little cubes» and later, in 1909, of «Cubism», the denomination finally becoming established. Thanks to the business sense of the German dealer Kahnweiler, Picasso had no longer any need to suffer from economic anxieties. In the summer of **1909,** in the company of his friend Fernande Olivier, he once more went to Horta de Ebro (Tarragona). Upon his return to Paris, he was already in the current of «analytic Cubism», in the autumn, he left the Bateau-Lavoir for a studio in the Boulevard de Clichy where he did Cubist sculpture and exhibited in the Tannhauser Gallery in Munich. In **1910,** he painted the surprising potraits of Vollard, Uhde and Kahnweiler, spent the summer in Cadaqués (Gerona) with Fernade Olivier and returned to Paris in the autumn. The tenacious dismemberment to which he subjected form gave an effective hermetism which to a certain extent led him away from the figurative vocation to which he was always to be faithful. In this way, and like Braque, he began his efforts to make his works more intelligible. The Autumn Salon ended by accepting the Cubists and exhibited Duchamp-Villon, Duchamp, Le Fresnaye, Gleizes, Léger, Le Faconnier, Picabia and Metzinger. Apollinaire criticised all those who imitated Picasso. In **1911,** he took part in exhibitions in Berlin, Amsterdam and New York. He spent the summer in Ceter

(Pyrenees) with Fernande and once more exhibited at the Tannhauser Gallery in Munich. In **1912** he took up pictorial Cubism as orienting guide-lines which were *real* and not illusionistic. He began to do *collages,* gluing diverse fragments together: bits of wallpaper, newspaper, netting, oilcloth, sand... On the strength of the *collage,* he arrived at «synthetic Cubism». In **1913,** Picasso's father, José Ruiz Blasco, died. For some time, his life with Fernande Olivier had become extremely difficult and Picasso had had a relationship with Eva Gouel —whose married name was Marcelle Humbert— having inserted her name in more than one of his Cubist works. He spent the summer in Ceret, where Juan Gris, Braque and Max Jacob were also to go. By **1914,** Cubism had become simpler, more decorative, colouristic and with large planes. Picasso went to live in meridional Avignon with Eva. The outbreak of the First' World War on August 2nd was a great blow to him and he saw many of his French friends called to ranks. He returned with Eva to Paris in November, where he devoted his efforts to sculpture and achieved sculptoric forms and principles which were to have wide reper-cussion on other sculptors. He took part in exhi-bions in Berlin, Dresden and New York. If anything was hard for Picasso it was being subjected to one single creative medium and in **1915** one could perceive among his Cubist drawings certain ones which rather than «ingresque», as they have been called, could be termed «proto-classical» in anticipation of Picassian «classicism» which was to become a fact five years later. Max Jacob, who had become converted to Christianity, was godfather to the baptism. Eva died in January **1916.** Picasso

Les Demoiselles d'Avignon

went to Montrouge near Paris. He made friends
with Erik Satie and Jean Cocteau. In **1917,** both
persuaded him to work for the famous Russian
Ballet, in particular for «Parade». In February, he
travelled to Rome with Cocteau to discuss it with
Diaghilev. Among the corps-de-ballet of this latter
he met the dancer Olga Kovlova and became
friends with both her and Stravinsky. He returned
to Paris after a month in Rome. «Parade» had its

debut in May, with practically no effect. Picasso spent the summer between Madrid and Barcelona, accompanying the Russian Ballet. In January **1918** Paul Guillaume's gallery was opened with an exhibition by Picasso and Matisse, prologued by Apollinaire. On the 12th July he married Olga the Russian dancer. He then began a more ordered and «social life». He moved to good lodgings in the Rue de la Boétie and spent the summer in Biarritz. He painted bathers, now not in the Cubist style. In **1919,** he travelled to London with Diaghilev's ballet. He worked for the «Three-Cornered Hat» and

Three musicians

spent the summer in Saint-Raphael (Cote d'Azur). In **1920** he collaborated in the ballet «Punchinello», spent the summer in Juan-les-Pins and launched his medular classicism, which was deeply Mediterranean and which is usually called his «neoclassical period». In **1921** he worked for Diaghilev on the ballet «Cuadro Flamenco». His son Pablo was born on the 4th February. He spent the summer in Fontainebleau. In **1922** he painted the canvas «L'après-midi d'un faun» for the Russian ballet, and was commissioned with Cocteau's «Antigone». In the summer of **1923** he went to see his mother in Cap d'Antibes. Diaghilev was still giving him work in **1924:** «Le train bleu» and «Mercure». He spent the summer in Juan-les-Pins. Surrealism came into being and one of Picasso's works was reproduced in the first number of the magazine «Révolution surréaliste». In the spring of **1925** he painted in Montecarlo, whilst he spent the summer in Juan-les-Pins. André Breton illustrated his important article «Le Surréalisme et la Peinture» with many of Picasso's creations. This was in the fourth number of «Révolution surréaliste». Picasso was not missing in the first exhibition of this new group which was held in the Pierre Gallery in Paris. However much he may have been criticised by the conservative tendencies of the time, Picasso's fame had already reached both transcendental and international dimensions. Eugenio d'Ors' prophecy therefore seemed to be on the way to fulfilment and even to attain unsuspectedly difficult goals. Whether Cubist or otherwise, his most important works of this period are: Les Demoiselles d'Avignon, Portrait of Ambroise Vollard, Portrait of Wilhelm Uhde, Portrait of Daniel-Henry Kahnweiler,

Woman with a Mandoline, The Aficionado, Woman in Nightshirt, Portrait of Olga, Woman Dressed in Spanish Style («La Salchichona»), Pierrot, Sergio Diaghilev and Alfred Salisberg —a drawing—, *Sleeping Villagers, Portrait of Igor Stravinsky* —drawing—, *The Three Musicians, Portrait of André Breton* —dry nib— *Pablito on a donkey, Pablito dressed as a Harlequin, Pablito dressed as a Pierrot,*

Till the End of the Spanish Civil War (1926-1939).

The «Cahiers d'Art», which were founded by Christian Zervos, appeared in **1926** and marked the beginning of an uninterrupted relationship with Picasso. Jean Cassou, Elie Faure and E. Tériade collaborated in them. As if incidentally, Picasso worked out a curvilinear, decorative and rhythmical cubism, like a path down which he could from time to time free himself from the strict rectitudes and right angles of «orthodox» Cubism. He held an anthological exhibition of his past twenty years in June in the Paul Rosenberg Gallery. In July, Waldemar George included sixty-four drawings by Picasso in «L'Amour de l'art», published in an independent volume at the end of the year under the title of «Picasso, dessins». He spent the summer in Juan-les-Pins. In October, he travelled to Barcelona. In January of **1927** he approached the young Marie Thérèse Walter —17-years-old— near Galeries Lafayette. A few months later his friendship with her was of a totally intimate nature. In July, he exhibited in the Paul Rosenberg Gallery. He spent the summer in Cannes with Olga and his son Pablo. He painted strange bathers with elephantine limbs and forms of impressive sur-realist expressionism, which were totally his own and as personal as they could be. He returned to París in the Autumn. In the Alfred Flechthein Gallery in Berlin, he exhibited four bronzes, twenty engravings, pastel drawings, water-colours and drawings from October to November. In the winter, he carried out the first of the engravings which were to illustrate Balzac's «Le Chef — d'oeuvre inconnu» commissioned by Vollard. At the end of this year and the beginning of **1928,** he exhibited in the Pierre Gallery in Paris. The theme of the minotaur which was to be so often portrayed in his work, appeared for the first time in January. He modelled in bronze his *Bather-Metamorphosis I* for casting. he renewed the deal which he had had since 1902 with Julio González, in search of techni-cal aid for the construction of the monument to Apollinaire. He was to learn the trade of metal-welding with him. He spent the summer in Dinard (Brittany) with Olga and Pablo and, surreptitiously, with Marie Thérèse Walter. He made sketches for sculptures. Once in Paris in Julio González's workshop, he carried out his first sculpture in metal wire. Wilhelm Uhde published «Picasso et la tradition française», pointing out the artist's impor-tance within the context of French art. He was still working in Julio's workshop at the beginning of **1929.** His tense relationship with Olga is reflected in several works which portray the aggressive head of a woman. Zervos published «Projets de Picasso pour un monument». He spent the summer in Dinard. **1930** began with more work in Julio González's workshop. He participated in the first exhibition of the Museum of Modern Art in Paris

Bust and palette

with fourteen works. Together with Derain, he exhibited in the Reinhardt Galleries, New York. He worked on a *Crucifixión* in which certain aspects of **Guernica** have been foreseen. He took part in the exhibition of collages in the Goemans Gallery in Paris and, with a preface by Aragón, he exhibited in the Arts Club in Chicago. A special number of «Documents» was devoted to him. He bought a country house in Boisgeloup, near Gisors and spent the summer in Juan-les-Pins. Upon his return to Paris, he housed Marie Thérèse Walter in the same street in which he lived with his wife, Olga. He worked on the exquisitely beautiful engravings commissioned by Albert Skira which were published the following year. He exhibited in the John

The Dream and Lie of Franco (I). Scene 1

Becker Gallery, New York. Eugenio d'Ors published «Pablo Picasso» and Gertrude Stein «Dix Portraits». He took part in the exhibition at the Rembrandt Gallery in New york and in January **1931,** the Valentine Gallery in New York organized the «Abstractions of Picasso» exhibition in the Harvard Society for Contemporary Art, in Cambridge with fifteen engravings from the «Metamorphoses of Ovid». Tristan Tzara published an article in «Cahiers d'Art» on the collages. In Julio González's workshop, he introduced common objects into his sculptures. He returned to curvilinear Cubism. He exhibited thirty-six works in the Alex Reid & Lefèvre Gallery in London. He turned a stable of the *château* at Boisgeloup into a sculpture workshop. Although he did not abandon the metal sculpture which he had been doing with Julio González, he now returned to modelling in clay and plaster. He worked in Boisgeloup and spent the summer in Juan-les-Pins. He did the engravings for the last part of the *Suite Vollard,* to a great extent under the influence of his affaire with Marie Thérèse. The engravings of the «Metamorphoses of Ovid» and Balzac's «Chef – d'oeuvre inconnu» were published. He exhibited in the Rosenberg Gallery, Paris. The Carnegie Institute awarded a prize to the portrait he had painted of Olga in 1918. During the first three months of **1932** he painted works under Marie Thérèse's influence. There was a large re-trospective exhibition in the Georges Petit Gallery with division of critical acclaim into revulsion and enthusiasm: Zervos published a special number of «Cahiers d'Art» upon this occasion. The exhibition was shown in the Zurich Künsthaus and was badly received. Jung identified it with schizophrenia and alienation. Olga and their son Pablo spent the

The Dream and Lie of Franco (I). Scene 3

The Dream and Lie of Franco (I). Scene 4

summer perhaps without Picasso in Juan-les-Pins. Picasso had to stay in Boisgeloup, surrounded by friends such as Kahnweiler, Raynal, Braque, Julio González, Leiris and Zervos, and where he carried on with his sculptures of women's heads inspired by Marie Thérèse Walter. Zervos published the first volume of his catalogue of Picasso's work, from 1895 to 1906. Twenty-eight volumes were to be published between 1932 and 1974. The Barcelona Museum received twenty of his works which had come from the Plandiura Collection. Picasso turned once more to the theme of the *Crucifixión,* interpreting Mathias Grünewald's famous one, a version which was reproduced in **1933** in the first number of «Minotaure». Together with Joseph Cornell, he exhibited in the Julien Levy Gallery in New York. He did numerous engravings from March 1933 onwards, devoting certain attention to the

The Dream and Lie of Franco (I). Scene 9

theme of the sculptor in his studio and, in some cases, attempting to identify with children's drawings, an attempt which was to be confirmed by his statement that it took him many years to achieve. He spent his holidays in Cannes with Olga and Pablo, travelling in grand style to Barcelona in his spectacular Hispano-Suiza and staying at the Ritz. He returned to Paris in September. His first mistress, Fernande Olivier, launched her book «Picasso and his friends», which was important in understanding the first years of the artist in Paris. Bernard Geiser published a detailed catalogue of Picasso's engravings and lithographs of 1899 to 1931. At the beginning of **1934,** the figure of Rembrandt begins to appear in some of his engravings. He exhibited in the Wadsworth Atheneum in Hartford (Connecticut). He carried out bull-fighting series, both in engravings, paintings and drawings. In the

The Dream and Lie of Franco (II). Scene 11

summer he travelled to Spain with Olga and Pablo, and watched bull-fights, passing through San Sebastián, Burgos, Madrid, Toledo, Zaragoza and Barcelona. He returned to Paris in September. Manuel Abril won the National Prize for Literature in 1934 for his «De la Naturaleza al Espíritu», which was published in 1935 and which is an open elogy and highly energetic defence of Picasso. In May **1935,** Picasso stopped painting until the following spring. He exhibited collages from 1912 to 1914 in the Pierre Gallery. He participated in the «Creators of Cubism» exhibition in the Galerie des Beaux-Arts» in Paris. He engraved the **Minotauromachy** (cf.) Marie Thérèse Walter was expecting a baby. Picasso could not get a divorce from Olga, on account of the legal dfficulties concerning the sharing out of their property, for his affaire with Marie Thérèse had begun when she was still legally under age, and in view of Picasso's Spanish nationality, which he would not give up even for this reason. He called Sabartés, who was living in South America, to come over and be his secretary. On the 5th October, Marie Thérèse gave birth to a little girl —María de la Concepción-Maïa, Maya— Picasso being godfather at her christening. He neither painted nor drew. He merely wrote. Alongside the surrealists he created poems following the method of «pure psychic automatism», some of which were published in the «Cahiers d'Art». In February, **1936,** he held a retrospective exhibition at the Esteva Gallery in Barcelona which was organized by ADLAN —Amigos de las Artes Nuevas—. The press write-ups were hostile to him, partly on account of the way in which the exhibition was politicized. It was hoped that he would support the Popular Front. Picasso did not attend

The Dream and Lie of Franco (II). Scene 12

the meetings although Sabartés did. Julio González, Miró, Dalí, Paul Eluard and Ramón Gómez de la Serna also did. Before going on to Bilbao, the same exhibition was held in Madrid and was prefaced by Guillermo de Torre. It was logically repudiated in conservative circles. Among those who praised it were Enrique Lafuente Ferrari and Eduardo Westerdahl who devoted a number of his «Gaceta de Arte» to Picasso. There was an exhibition of works between 1934 and 1935 in the Rosenberg gallery. In March, Picasso went to Juan-les-Pins with Marie Thérèse and Maya, where he was to work on the theme of the minotaur. Back in Paris, he worked on the illustrations to the «Natural History» by Buffon, which were not published until 1942. He joined the public ceremonies held in honour of the triumph of the Popular Front in France. The Spanish Civil War broke out on the 18th of July

The Dream and Lie of Franco (II). Scene 14

and Picasso opposed General Franco by appointing himself *Honorary* Director of the Prado Museum. He went to Mougins, near Cannes, in August. Dora Maar, whose surname was Markovich, was among those who visited him them. She was a photographer and the daughter of a Yugoslav architect and had known Picasso since the beginning of the year, having previously lived in Argentina and speaking fluent Spanish. Picasso came to know the pottery village of Vallauris with her and they soon became intimate. He left his studio in Boisgeloup and worked at Tremblay-sur-Mauldre. He exhibited fifty-seven works in the Zwemmer Gallery in London. From the 8th to the 9th of January, **1937,** he shut himself away to carry out the engravings for the **Dream and lies of Franco** (cf.) adding a poem as an autograph. The four final scenes of the second plate were finished on the 7th June. The

The Dream and Lie of Franco (II). Scene 15

edition was sold to obtain funds for the Spanish Republic. He managed to get a new studio with Dora Maar in the Rue des Grands-Augustins, in a 17th-century building. The government of the Spanish Republic commissioned a mural from him for their pavillion in the International Exhibition to be held in the month of June. He exhibited in the Valentine Gallery in New York. On the 26th April, the bombing raid on the village of Guernica took place. Picasso learned the news from friends and the press and thus decided to paint the mural with which he had been entrusted. On the 1st May he began the sketches for **Guernica.** He took part with thirty-two works in the «Masters of Independent Art» exhibition held at the Petit Palais. On the 12th of June, the Spanish Pavillion of the International Exhibition was inaugurated; it had been designed by José Luis Sert and Luis Lacasa. Although **Guernica** was already finished, he kept working on same subject right through the summer and autumn, making a sort of *a posteriori* sketches and other pictures. «Cahiers d'Art» published articles and poems on **Guernica** and the photos (cf.) of the execution process taken by Dora Maar. He went with her to Mougins. They returned to Paris in September. He travelled to Switzerland in October, where he was to meet Paul Klee, then seriously ill. He exhibited twenty-three works —dated from 1901 to 1937— in the Valentine gallery, New York and carried out the «Twenty Years in the Evolution of Picasso» exhibition (1903-1923) in the Jacques Seligmann & Co. Gallery, also in New York. Upon this occasion, the Museum of Modern Art of New York managed to acquire *Les Demoiselles d'Avignon* which was being shown to the public then. The «New York Times» published the manifesto which Picasso had written defending the Spanish Republic for the Congress of American Artists in New York. He exhibited twice in London at the Zwemmer Gallery and then in Chicago with Giorgio. In March **1938,** cocks begin to appear on his canvasses. He went to Mougins in the summer with Dora Maar, returning to Paris at the end of September. **Guernica** was also exhibited in Norway in the summer and then, from the 4th to the 29th of October, with more than sixty of his studies in the New Burlington Galleries in London, in aid of the Spanish Republic, the exhibition being repeated at the Whitechapel Gallery, London and in Leeds and Liverpool. There was a Matisse and Picasso exhibition in Boston Museum, and an exhibition in the Valentine Gallery, New York, of works from 1908 to 1934. On the 13th of January **1939,** Picasso's mother died in Barcelona. There were exhibitions in the Rosenberg Gallery, Paris and London. He took part in the collective of the Marie Harriman Gallery, New York. The «Picasso before 1910» exhibition was held in the Perls Gallery, New York. From the 5th to the 29th May, **Guernica** and its studies were exhibited at the Valentine Gallery, New York in aid of Spanish emigrants. The same exhibition went to the Stendhal Gallery from the 10th to 21st August in Los Angeles and from there to the Chicago Arts Club and the San Francisco Museum. All of it was shown in the retrospective exhibition of Picasso's work organized by the Museum of Modern Art, New York in November. There was the «Picasso in English Collections» exhibition at the London Gallery, London. In July he went with Dora Maar to Antibes. Ambroise

Vollard died in an accident on the 22nd July and Picasso went to Paris for the funeral of his old friend. He returned to the south with Sabartés and painted in Antibes. He went back to Paris on August 25th. The Second World War broke out on the 1st September. Picasso went to Royan, near Bordeaux, with Dora Maar and Sabartés; Marie Thérèse and Maya were living too close to avoid embarrassing situations arising between Picasso's two mistresses. The local authorities treated Picasso as a foreigner and he was obliged to obtain the corresponding residence permit in Paris. From the 15th November **1939** to the 7th January **1940** the great retrospective exhibition «Picasso, Forty Years of his Art» was held in the Museum of Modern Art, New York in collaboration with the Chicago Art Institute, with 344 works and the **Guernica** with its studies. Throughout **1940,** the exhibition went in different versions to Chicago, Saint Louis, Boston, San Francisco, Cincinnati, Cleveland, New Orleans, Minneapolis and Pittsburgh.

Twenty-one years more of intense creativity and life (1940-1961)

Apart from the foregoing, along the same formal lines, he set up his studio in Royan in **1940.** He still made sporadic trips to Paris. He exhibited water-colours and gouaches in the Yvonne Zervos Gallery in Paris. On the 14th of July, the Germans entered Paris and on the 23rd, Picasso was back in Royan. He returned to Paris with Sabartés on the 25th August. He left his flat in the Rue de la Boétie, and went to live in that in the Rue des Grands-

The Germinal sketch for Guernica　**1**

Agustins. He rejected the favours offered to him by the Germans and gave them photos of **Guernica.** French soldiers destroyed some of Picasso works in the Boisgeloup studio. He turned down invitations to go to countries such as the United States or Mexico, because he preferred to stay in France. In January **1941** he wrote the farce «Le Désir attrapé par la queue» («Desire caught by the tail») published in 1944. He turned once more to «automatic» surrealist poetry and filled a whole page with false doggerel. In spring, Marie Thérèse and Maya returned to Paris and were visited at weekends by Picasso. He turned again to sculpture. All the strategic metals having been confiscated by the Germans, he had to cast his bronze sculptures clandestinely by night. On the 27th March **1942** his friend Julio González died. Maurice Vlaminck accused Picasso in the review «Comoedia» of being responsible for the degradation of French painting. André Lhote defended him in the same review. Picasso collaborated in the clandestine review «Les lettres françaises». Buffon's «Natural History» was published with 31 acquatints of animals. In **1943** he worked on sculptures with common objects: *Bull's Head* with the handlebars and seat of a bicycle, and did modelling in clay. In May he met the painter Françoise Gilet and saw her for two months until she left for the south of France. When she returned in September, she visited Picasso's studio more often. His Jewish friends were persecuted by the Germans. Zervos had to flee. On the 5th March **1944,** Max Jacob died in a concentration camp. A reading of «Le Désir attrapé par la queue» was carried out under the direction of Albert Camus, friends such as Jean-Paul Sartre, Simone de Beauvoir and Dora Maar each reading their parts and Georges Hugnet composing the musical background. Back in his studio he revealed to those present that he had been inspired by an original of Alfred Jarry's, called «Ufu cocu». In August he moved with Maya and Marie Thérèse to the Boulevard Henri IV. Paris was freed on the 25th August. He returned to the studio in the Grands-Augustins. In October he joined the Communist Party. He took part in the Autumn Salon with a special room —the so-called «Liberation» exhibition— at which his first public recognition by French artists was offered to him. However, he was violently discussed by students at the Fine Arts

School, and by conservative-minded people for his membership of the Communist Party. The National Committee of Authors supported him, with the signatures of Mauriac, Valéry, Aragón, Eluard, Sartre and Duhamel. At the beginning of **1945,** he started *The Ossuary* to a certain extent a continuation of **Guernica** and in which expressionism and echoes of Cubism mingle. He still painted dramatized still-lifes which were meant to signify the Hardships of the past German occupation. There was an exhibition in the Buchholz Gallery in New York on the 27th February to the 17th March, with works from a private collection. He kept on working on the *Ossuary,* which was intended to be related to the feeling he experienced from photos of the camp at Dachau, although these latter were published once the work had been conceived of and was well on the way to development. Ramón Gómez de la Serna published his «Completa y verídica historia de Picasso y el Cubismo». The Tenth Congress of the French Communist Party paid homage to Picasso, but recommended artists to follow socialist dogmatic realism. He painted the back-cloth to the ballet «Le Rendez-vous». The «Free Picasso» exhibition was held from the 20th June to the 18th July at the Louis Carré Gallery in Paris. He left for Antibes with Dora Maar. Françoise Gilet went to Brittany, but Picasso booked a room for her in Golfe-Juan almost at the same time as he acquired a house in Ménerbes in exchange for a still-life, only to give it over in property to Dora Maar. He returned to Paris in August. He figured in the Autumn Salon with two Paintings. In Fernand Mourlot's workshop, he began a portrait of Françoise as the start of a series of more than 200 lithographs which he was to carry out in the next three and a half years. This medium allowed him to reflect, image by image, his continual change, so characteristic of him. He became enthusiastic about the most diverse graphic techniques. He met Françoise Gilet again in November. There was a Picasso and Matisse exhibition at the Victoria and Albert Museum, London. At the end of 1945 he began his *Monument to the Spaniards*. From the 15th February to the 15th March **1946,** he took

6 *The second approach to a general symbological lucubration (Detail)*

part in the «Art and Resistance» exhibition held at the National Museum of Modern Art in Paris. Françoise Gilet, convalescing from a fracture of the elbow, left for Golfe-Juan where Picasso was to meet up with her. They returned to Paris at the end of April and began to live together. He began a series of portraits of her under the common denominator of *Flower Woman*. She was also to serve as a subject for lithographs. He exhibited 19 pictures in the Louis Carré Gallery in Paris. At the beginning of July, he left with Françoise for the house he had bought for Dora Maar in Ménerbes. Marie Thérèse wrote to him daily. He travelled to Cap d'Antibes with Françoise in an attempt to flee

The second approach to a general symbological lucubration **6**

from this epistolar persecution. Gertrude Stein died on the 27th July, having for some time been distant from Picasso and their old friendship having been interrupted. He went to Golfe-Juan with Françoise. He undertook 22 paintings on wooden panels for the walls of Antibes Museum, the Grimaldi palace which changed its name to the Picasso Museum. Françoise and Picasso attended the Cannes Film Festival. There, André Breton, upon his return from the United States, reproached Picasso with having joined the Communist Party. He returned to Paris at the end of November with Françoise. Jaime Sabartés published «Portraits et Souvenirs». In March **1947** Picasso carried out six versions of Lucas Cranach's *Bathsheba*. He donated 10 works to the National Museum of Modern Art in Paris. Previously, French museums had only poss- essed three of his works: two in Grenoble and one in Jeu de Paume. On the 15th May, his first child by Françoise, Claude, was born. He left with both of them in June for Golfe-Juan. In August he began to make pottery in Vallauris in Georges Ramié's workshop, making more than 2,000 pieces until the following year, giving new life to the crafts industry of the village. Juan Larrea's **«Guernica: Pablo Picasso»** was published in New York, with photos by Dora Maar and introduction by Alfred H. Barr, Jr. Picasso designed the décor for «King Oedipus» by Sophocles which was put on at the Champs Elysées Theatre. He lived almost continually in the Midi. In **1948,** he made the documentary film «A Visit to Picasso» which was in Vallauris in the Picasso Museum. The 125 lithographs were finished which had been started in 1945 for Pierre Reverdi's «Chant des Morts». He finished 41 engravings for Góngora's «Vingt poèmes». He went to Galloise, a town near Vallauris, with Françoise in the summer. He was awarded the «Medaille de la Recon- naissance Française». He travelled to Poland with Eluard to attend the Congress of Intellectuals for Peace. He visited Wroclaw, Auschwitz, Cracow and Warsaw. He painted Ilya Ehrenburg's portrait. The President of the Polish Republic decorated him. He returned to Vallauris at the begining of September. In October, he travelled to Paris. In November he exhibited 149 pieces of pottery at the Maison de la Pensée in Paris. He kept on with the lithographs inspired by Françoise. In January **1949,** «Les Sculptures de Picasso» was published with text by Daniel Henri Kahnweiler. The lithograph of a dove was used for a poster to the Peace Congress inaugurated in Paris in April, and thenceforth became called the *Peace Dove*. The Philadelphia Museum awarded this work the «Pennell Memorial Medal». Mérimée's «Carmen» was published with 38 engravings by Picasso. The «Pablo Picasso: recent work» exhibition was held in the Buchholz Gallery, New York from the 8th March to the 2nd April. On the 19th April, Paloma the daughter of Françoise and Picasso, was born. He did lithographs with «automatic» writing. In spring he returned to Vallauris and rented an old drug-store as studio and pottery warehouse. He exhibited 64 works in the Maison de la Pensée in the month of July. In the autumn, he devoted himself more to sculpture. In the winter of **1950** he carried out the sculpture *Pregnant Woman* in clay and later cast in bronze —1955 and 1959. He painted works portraying Claude and Paloma, and made new versions of works by Courbet and El Greco. He worked with objects which he had «found» and continued with his pottery. On the 25th June, the Korean war broke out. One of the three casts of the *Man with a Ram* was kept in Vallauris. In October he attended the Second World Peace Conference, held in Sheffield (England), the poster for which was designed by Picasso with a dove in flight. In November, he was awarded the Lenin Peace Prize. From November to June **1951,** he carried out an exhibition of sculptures and drawings in the Maison de la Pensée, which was prefaced by Louis Aragón. On the 18th January, he painted *The Korean Executions* against the United States, a work which was to feature in the May

Salon in Paris. He was turned out of his flat in the Rue de la Boétie and went to live in one in the Rue Gay Lussac. He returned to Vallauris with Françoise, and continued with his sculptures done with «found» objects. Threatened with eviction from his Paris home, he was forced to return there and stay in it. The same year (1951) he attended the IV Congress of Intellectuals for Peace in Rome. From the 19th February to the 15th March **1952,** he held an exhibition at the Curt Valentin Gallery in New York. He was still concerned about the Korean war and decided to decorate a non-denominational chapel in Vallauris, as a temple to peace. To this end, he carried out more than two hundred and fifty studies. At the end of October he travelled alone to Paris. His relationship with Françoise was not going smoothly. In December, he returned to Vallauris and worked on the panels for the peace temple which was not to be installed until 1954. He wrote «Quatre petites filles» at La Galloise, which was a play in six acts. In January **1953** he travelled to Paris. From the 30th January to the 9th April, there was an exhibition «Le cubisme 1907-1914» in the National Museum of Modern Art, Paris, in which Les demoiselles d'Avignon featured. He returned to Vallauris in February. Stalin died on the 5th March. Picasso drew his portrait for «Les Lettres Françaises» and met with the disapproval of the French Communist Party. From May to July there was the great retrospective exhibition in the National Gallery of Modern Art in Rome, the exhibition being repeated in Milan in September with the addition of **Guernica** and The Korean Executions. In June, there was a retrospective exhibition in Lyon Museum. In

Fourth, oil-paint version of the neighing horse's head **9**

August, he travelled to Perpignan with Maya to attend a bull-fight in Colliure. At Perpignan he met the divorcée Jacqueline Roque. In September, the Communist Party of Ceret paid homage to him. He returned to Vallauris. Françoise left him, taking with her their children Claude and Paloma. In November he began the series of drawings on the painter and his model. Sabartés donated his library on Picasso and the works he possessed in Barcelona to the Malaga Museum. From the 13th December to the 20th February **1954,** there was a great retrospective exhibition in Sao Paulo with **Guernica.** In April 1954, he met the young woman Silvette David, who was to be his model for forty drawings and paintings. In June, he painted the *Portrait of Madame,* that is Jacqueline Roque. In

July, there was an exhibition at the Maison de la Pensée with works from the periods 1900-1914 and 1950-1954, some from the Gertrude Stein Collection and from Russian museums. He went to bull-fights in Vallauris with Jacqueline Roque, Penrose, Cocteau, Prévert and Françoise Gilet and their children. He met Jacqueline unexpectedly in Perpignan with Maya and returned to Paris with her to live together there. He saw Derain, Matisse, Maurice-Raynal and Henri Laurens die. He painted new versions of Eugène Delacroix's *Women of Algiers*. Olga died on the 11th February **1955** in Cannes, having been his legitimate wife. He travelled with Jacqueline to Rosellon (Provence) in May. From May to June, there was an exhibition in the Marlborough Gallery, London. From June to October, there was a retrospective exhibition from 1900 to 1905 with **Guernica** in the Museum of Decorative Arts, and one with graphic works at the National Library, Paris. In summer 1955, the film «Le mystère Picasso» was made by Henri Georges Clouzot. Picasso bought «La Californie», a nineteenth-century villa near Cannes overlooking Golfe-Juan and Antibes. He painted a version of *Lola de Valencia* by Manet, using Jacqueline as a model. Between the 25th October 1955 and April **1956, Guernica** was exhibited in Cologne, Paris, Hamburg, Munich, Stockholm, Brussels and Amsterdam. In 1956 Picasso turned once more to his old theme of bathers, making sculptures out of some of his paintings. His seventy-fifth birthday was celebrated in Vallauris. Ilya Ehrenburg commemorated it in Moscow with an exhibition. On the 22nd November, he protested with other intellectuals to the Communist Party for Russian repression in Hungary. «Le Monde» published their manifesto. From March to April **1957,** there was an exhibition at the Louise Leiris Gallery in Paris. From the 4th May to the 8th September, their was an exhibition to commemorate his seventy-fifth birthday in the Museum of Modern Art, New York. From the 6th July to the 2nd September, there was an exhibition in the Réattu Museum in Arles. From the 17th August to the 30th December, he painted more than forty versions of Velázquez's *Meninas* in «La Californie». UNESCO entrusted him with the decoration of the delegates room at their Paris headquarters. After several essays and studies, he chose the theme of the *Fall of Icarus*. From the 8th March to the 8th June **1958,** there was an exhibition of his pottery in the Maison de la Pensée. He showed his murals for UNESCO in a state school in Vallauris. He painted several versions of Cannes Bay from his study in «La Californie». In September, he bought the Château at Vauvenargues, dating from the 14th century, on mount Sainte-Victoire (Aix-en-Provence), which had so often been painted by Cézanne. From February **1959** onwards, he was to work in the château at Vauvenargues. He painted 21 oil-paintings with versions of the wrongly called «bobo de Murillo» when it was really a certain mixture of some of Velázquez's works —*Sebastián Morra,* to be precise— and Murillo's *Child* in the Louvre. From the 22nd May to the 27th June, there was an exhibition of his *Meninas* in the Louise Leiris Gallery, Paris. On the 5th June, the monument to Apollinaire was inaugurated, with a head of Dora Maar, in Saint-Germain-des-Prés, París. He spent the summer in «La Californie». In February **1960** he painted nudes. He returned to

10 *Third approach to the general lucubration (Detail)*

the theme of the painter and his model, which he was not to leave for a long time. From the 15th June to the 13th July, there was a lino-cut exhibition at the Louise Leiris Gallery. From the 6th July to the 18th September, there was a retrospective exhibition at the Tate Gallery, London. He began sketches for the decoracion of the College of Architects in Barcelona. From November to December, there was an exhibition in the Gaspar Gallery in Barcelona. This was the first of a series of others which were to be held in the following years. Camilo José Cela published a monographic paper on «The Papers of Sao Ardemans» dedicated to Picasso. On the 2nd March **1961,** Picasso married Jacqueline Roque at Vallauris. In June he moved to his new home in Notre-Dame-de-Vie, near Mougins. On the 25th October, he was eighty. His birthday was commemorated in Vallauris and in the UCLA Art Gallery, Los Angeles. Many Spaniards have commemorated the occasion by publishing articles and essays.

Third approach to the general lucubration **10**

The Fertile Output of the Final Stretch of His Life (1962-1973)

From the 26th January to the 24th February **1962,** there was an exhibition in the Louise Leiris Gallery. From the 25th April to the 12th May, there was an exhibition in New York organized by nine art galleries. On the 1st May he once more received the Lenin Peace Prize. From the 14th May to the 18th September, there was a commemorative exhibition for his eightieth birthday in the Museum of Modern Art, New York. Serge Lifar asked him to do the décor for the ballet «Icarus». He painted a version of David's *Rape of the*

Sabines, and also did countless engravings. There was an exhibition in the Museum of Western Art in Tokyo with the «preparatory» sketches to **Guernica** and a tapestry of this work —3,048 × 6,706— done in 1955. On the 9th March **1963,** the Picasso Museum was inaugurated in Barcelona. His friends Braque and Cocteau died. From the 11th January to the 16th Febrary **1964,** there was the exhibition «Picasso and Man» at the Toronto Art Gallery which later went on to Montreal. From the 15th January to the 15th February there was an exhibition in the Louise Leiris Gallery. Françoise Gilot, with the collaboration of Carlton Lake, published her «My Life with Picasso». From the 23rd May to the 5th July, there was a retrospective exhibition in the Museum of Modern Art, Tokyo which later went on to Kioto and Nagoya. The Spanish Government acquired three canvasses by Picasso of the *Painter and His Model,* which are today in the Museum of Contemporary Art and which were to feature in the Spanish pavillion of the World Fair in New York. From the 22nd June to the 15th September, there was the exhibition «Picasso and the Theatre» in the Musée des Grands-Augustins in Toulouse. Picasso made his last trip to Paris in November for an operation for stomach-ulcer in the American hospital at Neuilly. In November **1966,** the French Government organized a retrospective exhibition of Picasso's works in the Grand Palais and the Petit Palais, with a collection of more than 700 works. In **1967** Picasso turned down the French Legion of Honour. He was evicted from his flat in the Rue des Grands-Augustins. From the 9th June to the 13th August, there was an exhibition of sculpture and pottery in the Tate

Gallery, London, which later went on to the Museum of Modern Art, New York, from the 11th October to the lst January **1968.** On the 13th February **1969,** Jaime Sabartés died. Picasso donated the *Meninas* series to Barcelona in memory of Sabartés. From the 28th February to the 23rd March, there was an exhibition in the Louise Leiris Gallery. From the 16th March to the 5th October, he did 347 engravings which were largely erotic and were exhibited from the 18th December to the 1st January **1969** in the Louise Leiris Gallery. Sixteen engravings of «La Celestina» were published with text by Picasso in Gustave Gili's «El Entierro del Conde de Orgaz». In January **1970,** Picasso's family in Barcelona donated all the works by the artist they possessed to Barcelona Museum. From the 1st May to the 1st October, there was an exhibition of his latest work in the Papal Palace at Avignon. On the 12th May, fire destroyed the Bateau-Lavoir of Picasso's youth. From the 18th October to the 29th November, there was a retrospective exhibition «Picasso, the master-engraver» in the Museum of Modern Art, New York. From the 15th December 1970 to the 2nd February **1971,** the «Cubist Epoch» exhibition was held at the Los Angeles County Museum of Art, which was later to go on to the New York Metropolitan Museum from the 7th April to the 7th June. From the 16th December 1970 to the 1st March 1971, there was the «Four Americans in Paris» exhibition, the Gertrude Stein Collection and that of her family, in the Museum of Modern Art, New York. From the 23rd April to the 5th June 1971, there was an exhibition of Picasso's latest works in the Louise Leiris Gallery. On the occasion of his ninetieth birthday, there was an exhibition in the Louvre. He was still working at Mougins in 1972, in particular on engravings and drawings. From the 23rd January to the 2nd April, there was the «Picasso and the Collection of the Museum of Modern Art» exhibition in New York. From the 1st December **1972,** to the 3rd January **1973,** there was the great exhibition of his last works in the Louise Leiris Gallery. He donated sculpture in metal wire to the Museum of Modern Art, New York. From the 24th January to the 24th February 1973, there was an exhibition of 156 engravings —from 1970 to 1972— in the Louise Leiris Gallery. Picasso died on the 8th April 1973 in Mougins. He was buried on the 10th in the gardens of his château in Vauvenargues.

GUERNICA

Prolegomenon and history

Until very recently, there were not enough known data with which the «official» history of **Guernica** could be documented[2].

When the Second Spanish Republic was declared on the 14th April 1931, Picasso had already been resident in France for a good number of years, not exactly as an expatriate, but removed from the country which he was always to consider his home. He lived in the light of Parisian artistic life which offered him greater international projection for the spectacular market his works were to open up and even a personal way of life which would have been ostracized both in Barcelona and Madrid by the right-thinking sectors of society which were doubtless both ruled and ruling.

The Republic came to Spain together with an optimistic spirit of cultural renovation, but conservatism remained powerful everywhere: in the Press, art criticism, among collectors, in art galleries and a long etc., which always affects the commerce of ideas and works of art. For this reason, the innovators were obliged to live in a constant and generalized climate of incomprehen-

---

[2] Javier Tussell made this known in «El País», 17th, 18th, 19th, 22nd, 23rd and 24th of September 1981 and later in «Guernica-Legado Picasso», October 1981; Tussell, as Director General of Fine Arts, Archives and Libraries, has handled Luis Araquistain's, who was Ambassador to the Republic in Paris, and it has recently been acquired by the Ministry of Culture.

sion. The refined sensibility of the painter Juan de Echevarría was to speedily pose the problem in four important articles[3], which referred chiefly to the Museum of Modern Art, in terms which almost —or entirely— may be literally applied today to its successor, the Spanish Museum of Contemporary Art. On discussing the policy of acquisitions, Echevarría was to assert that «With the same sums that had been spent so far, we could have enriched our Museum with works of the above-mentioned schools: Impressionism, Post-Impressionism, Cubism... by buying at ridiculously low prices. But the same money (Echevarría goes on to say) could have bought us a series of Picasso's at unheard-of prices. I myself brought three works of the great Spanish painter to Spain back in 1905 for he wished to sell them at a hundred pesetas a piece. Of the three, I managed to sell only one to a friend. This was when Picasso sold a lot of 30 works, drawings and paintings, among which were the most important of his Blue Period, for the sum of two thousand francs if my memory does not fail me, for he was then living in poverty in Montmartre in the Place Ravignan. «And let it not be argued that Picasso was unknown in Madrid, for he was here it so happened at that time and exhibited in the National Exhibition. I could not say whether in the chamber of horrors or on the stairs, but in any case, in one or the other of these places...» «...these were places of honour for the experts at that time». Echevarría was to die in the same year (1931), whilst the Republican Government was in

---

[3] With others of his, I reprinted them in my paper «Juan de Echevarría», Madrid, 1974. They appeared in «Crisol», 23rd and 30th April and 12th and 26th May 1931.

doubt as to whether to appoint him Head-Keeper of the Prado Museum or of the National Museum of Modern Art. Two Years later, as Director General of Fine Arts, Ricardo Orueta attempted to hold a Picasso exhibition in Madrid, but before his plan could be carried out, he wished to know whether Picasso was still Spanish or not. The great writer, Salvador de Madariaga, the Spanish Ambassador in Paris, told him that he was, although he had never accepted invitations sent him for receptions, lunches and dinners and that he did not even see to his personal phone calls, thus considering «Picasso's behaviour to me personally and to the Ambassador of his country frankly unmannerly». With this, Orueta «Totally rejected the project». It might be said by the way that this fact perhaps proves several points: Picasso's distaste for diplomatic and salon gatherings, whether under the auspices of Madariaga or otherwise; his refusal to thrive through approaches to the new political ethos of the Republic[4], and, how history may be changed by the mistrust of those with diplomatic «good manners», thus losing perhaps even the possibility of the return of an exceptional artist to his country, or at the very least, jeopardising a closer relationship with him. This hypothesis is valid in that in those days of 1933, nobody realised that the Civil War was going to break out in 1936 and even less what its results were to be.

That the Republic could not erradicate prevailing conservatism in the field of fine arts was also to be proved by the polemics on the occasion on

---

[4] Some time before this, in certain declarations to Kahnweiler, he told him that he was a monarchist, for there was a monarchy in Spain...

12 *Fourth attempt at a general lucubration (Detail)*

the award of the medal of honour at the National
Exhibition in 1934[5]. Both within and outside Spain,
Picasso's followers were restricted in those years to
an intellectual elite of critics, dealers and collectors, who were indeed loudly outspoken in favour
of him as likewise increasingly heeded and trium-
phant, although a minority. In his book «De la
Naturaleza al Espíritu» —National Prize for Literature in 1934 and printed in 1935, which was a sort of
Pandora's chest of Spanish art of the time—
Manuel Abril was to defend Picasso against his
«Obstinate detractors». Panegyrists and detractors
tore at each others' throats at the exhibitions
organized by ADLAN (Amigos de las Artes Nuevas)
in Madrid, Bilbao and Barcelona in 1936, politics
even interfering whith their opinions (see biogra-
phic data).

When the Spanish Civil War broke out on July

---

[5] By means of a truly democratic system and by an overwhelming
majority of votes, this was awarded to Marceliano Santa María,
against José Gutiérrez-Solana who was the great loser, although he
competed with the *End of the World, The Chemist's Backroom, Slum
House* and Young Lady Bull-Fighters. In spite of the way in which we
may today read this story and that we might be led to believe
otherwise, the fact is that conservatism prevailed everywhere. See, for
example, in the biography given on Picasso, how his works were
received in 1932 in Paris and Zurich.

Fourth attempt at a general lucubration **12**

18th, 1936, the painter José Renau, Director General of Fine Arts, decided «de motu propio» to draw Picasso over to the cause of the Popular Front to see what the painter could do for it. The Popular Front was then supported by many intellectuals of the French and European cultural avant-garde. In September, the President of the Republic, Manuel Azaña, signed the decree by which Picasso was appointed Honorary Director of the Prado Museum, an appointment which Picasso never took up, although he was able to win over even the most recalcitrant enemy of such a brilliant appointment. Renau saw Picasso in Paris towards the end of 1936 in order to discuss with the Ambassador, Luis Araquistain, how to organize the Spanish Republic's participation in the «Exposition Internationale des Arts et Techniques dans la Vie Moderne» which was planned by France in 1929 and developed by the French Ministry of Commerce and Industry, to be inaugurated on the 24th

May 1937 with the participation of 44 countries, the profits for which were to be distributed on the 25th November of the same year. They decided to send a Spanish delegation and appointed the architects Luis Lacasa and José Luis Sert. In February 1937, José Gaos was appointed by decree to the post of general commissar of the Spanish pavillion; later, Gassol and José María Ucelay were to collaborate with him on an equal footing, and as adjoints, Max Aub —the cultural attaché of the Spanish Embassy— and José Luis Vaamonde. We do not know whether officially or merely with official backing, but a month before, José Bergamín and perhaps also with direct participation from Max Aub and José Gaos, had commissioned a mural from Picasso for the Spanish pavillion which was to be erected in the Trocadero Gardens. The Mural was to be on any subject and its title and theme were to be specified later; it was to be done at the same time as he undertook the engravings which were to be the *Dream and Lie of Franco* series (cf.) Picasso began this latter work straight away, although it was to be finished much later, whilst he put off work on the mural day after day.

The historical Biscayan town of Guernica was bombed and machine-gunned on the 26th April by the German Air Force which was fighting with Franco's so-called «national» army. The news was given on the 29th in «The Times» and, on the 30th in «Ce Soir», with spectacular echoes in view of the fact that the ferocious attack was witnessed by a group of foreign journalists who were «accidentally» in Guernica. Through this press, or rather through his Spanish friends —Bergamín amongst them— Picasso learned of the dramatic event and was at last spurred to begin his mural, taking as the *germinal motif* for the working pending this bellicose genocide. This was not the only one of the Spanish Civil War and nobody at the time could suspect that it would only be the first of many which were to be culminated in 1945 in Hiroshima and Nagasaki, thus putting an end to a no less appalling World War. Thus, on the 1st May, Picasso began the first sketches (cf.) for his great canvas.

On the 28th May, Max Aub paid him for the yet unfinished work, as stipulated in a letter of the same date: «I came to an agreement with Picasso this morning. Despite our friend's reluctance to accept any subvention from the Embassy for painting **Guernica,** for he donates this work to the Spanish Republic, I have insistently reiterated the desire of the Spanish Government to pay at least the expenses caused by the work. I have managed to convince him and to this effect I have signed a cheque to the value of 150.000 French francs, for which he has signed the corresponding receipt. Although this sum has more of a symbolic nature in view of the priceless value of the work in question, it nonetheless represents practically the acquisition of same on behalf of the Republic. I believe this formula was the most suitable in order to claim the right to ownership of the above-mentioned work.»[6] **Guernica** was not to be trans-

---

[6] From what Javier Tussell has given us to believe (see the beginning of this chapter) one can hardly explain the fact that the figure of 150.000 francs should be considered «symbolic» in May 1937, for it was 15% of the total cost of the Spanish pavillion, some nine times more than the maximum price which Picasso had received till then, even for his best paid works. Strangely, in 1965, Max Aub was to write to Renau stating that **Guernica** had been paid, although «with

15 *Fifth attempt at a general lucubration*

the condition that the work continued to be his (i. e. Picasso's)», when really things were quite different and nobody knew the truth better than he did. The expenses for **Guernica** feature among others of the Spanish Embassy in Paris, dating only between October 1936 and May 1937, which amounted to 4.300.000 French francs —at the then current rate— and which were received by Spanish and foreign supporters of the Republic, personages such as Arthur Koestler, Pietro Nenni, Buñuel and the painter Luis Quintanilla. Zealous of his moral duties, Luis Araquistain requested from his Minister of State, Alvarez del Vayo, the receipt signed by Picasso on the 28th May 1937 and obtained as a reply that during the evacuation of Barcelona in 1939, he was unable to guard the archives of his Ministry, thus signing a certificate, which in principle fits in with what Max Aub wrote, and without for a moment doubting that «this friend (Picasso), should we one day recover the Republic, will ratify the donation he gave to the Republican Government of **Guernica**». And Araquistain did not stop there. Similarly in 1953, he was to write to Picasso reminding him of the facts: that the «symbolic» figure paid «implied and confirmed in itself your wish to make a donation of the picture to the Republic». It was logical that «the work should be in your hands and should not have fallen into those of present-day Spain, where it would probably have been destroyed in an «auto da fe» on account of its political and historical significance»; he also wrote «it may happen that another historical alternative will come about, not a revival of the Republic of 1936; that is to say, a constitutional and democratic Monarchy», which would have to be accepted by the painter and, in which case «you would have no other option, my friend Picasso, but to go to

ferred to its destination until the 4th June, to figure with two other sculptures by Picasso and certain works by Julio González, Alberto Sánchez and Juan Miró, plus the mercury fountain by the American Alexander Calder. But the inauguration of the Spanish pavillion of the exhibition by the Ambassador, Angel Ossorio y Gallardo, had to wait until the 12th July. Ossorio had replaced Araquistain and **Guernica** seemed poor and «unimpressive» to him. He did not seem to like Picasso's greatest canvas much, perhaps being the first person responsible for the fact that, upon that occasion or in its later exile, the Republic did not take possession of the work and left it in Picasso's hands.

What is quite certain is that it was not long before there was argument over the work commissioned from Picasso and his «interpretation» of the Guernica raid. As Manuel Llano Gorostiza has written, the Painter Julián Tellaeche (1884-1960) and a handful of Basque politicians tried to get **Guernica** replaced by works by Aurelio Arteta (1879-1940), the author of an indeed splendid triptych on the Spanish Civil War which represented in succession, *The Front* —soldiers defenceless in the face of the doubtlessly German Air Force—, *The Exodus* —of Basques in small fishing-vessels— and *The Rearguard* a young mother lying dead beside the corpse of her child. This happened between Spaniards of the same side. But on the other hand, as far as we know, Paris did not ac-

---

Madrid to take up that post and to hang up **Guernica** personally in the Picasso Room of a Prado Museum of which you would be the new of the process of **Guernica** taken by Dora Maar, were even paid by the Government of the Spanish Republic.

82

claim **Guernica** either with the astonishment and enthusiasm it was to later (not immediately) produce everywhere. Herschel B. Chipp —«Guernica-Picasso's Legacy»— tells us how the Spanish pavillion was ignored by the monthly catalogues and the exhibition's inaugural publicity. According to Le Corbusier, **Guernica** «merely saw the backs of the visitors, for these felt repelled by the painting». The public walked around the exhibition dazzled by the optimistic mirage which technological progress seemed to offer them, whilst the Spanish pavillion and, with it, **Guernica** showed no more than the terrible image of the war which was already staining part of Europe with blood. The German guide to the exhibition attacked «degenerate» art lengthily and, without expressly quoting **Guernica,** attacked it by calling it the work of a madman, a disorderly array of corpses, suitable for a young child. Not even Chipp's zeal for research has brought us information of too many discussions among advanced intellectuals, the directly favourable comments he mentions on this work being very few more; all this on a work which today at last is surrounded by a truly enormous bibliography. This proves conclusively how much grey matter Picasso accumulated in it and how it moved the minds of others.

The opinion of the normal spectator or common criticism is by no means represented in the important contents of the monographic number which «Cahiers d'Art» —No 4-5—, Paris 1937 , dedicates to **Guernica,** with texts by Zervos, Jean Cassou, Georges Durthuit, Pierre Mabille, Paul Eluard, Michel Leiris, José Bergamín, Juan Larrea and the seven photographs of other states of the work taken by

25 *The first of another series of different versions of the mother and dead child*

Dora Maar. **Guernica** did not deserve reproduction rights in the «Livre d'or officiel de l'Exposition Internationale des Arts et Techniques...», published in June 1938. It was not even mentioned in the brief review dedicated in it to the Spanish pavillion, whilst —what a contrast!— Germany took up considerable space with a large portrait of Hitler and Spain was missing from the final list of nations taking part. For the writers of this «Official Golden Book», the Exhibition had been «la manifestation du génie de la France». The ex-member of parliament, Jean Locquin, was right when he said that «the year 1937 would mark a great date in the history of the arts, of taste, of labour and of human thought», but what he perhaps never supposed was that this would be true for a quite different reason to those he must have had in mind. Even in 1947 (see the Picasso biography) ten years after the painting and exhibiting of **Guernica,** Picasso only had three works in French museums. This is because, no-

Second differentiated version of the mother with the dead **36**
child

where, not even in France which is always ahead in
these matters, is genius within the immediate
grasp of all. One thing is the promoting mechanisms of the truly powerful contemporary élites,
and a quite different one «consecrated» culture,
that of the society which depends upon it. In
agreement with Picasso and on account of the
needs of the Republican Government, **Guernica**
left France. From the 4th to the 29th October
1938 it was exhibited in the new Burlington Gallery
in London, being visited by only three thousand
people and by twelve thousand in its subsequent
exhibition at the Whitechapel in the East End.
Moreover, **Guernica** was also showered with re-

vulsion from conservative critics in England, the conspicuously avant-garde critics being divided over it.

In May 1939, it was in New York and in August at the Stendhal Gallery in Los Angeles. This coincided with the outbreak of the Second World War whilst it was being exhibited at the San Francisco Museum. On the 3rd October, the **Guernica** exhibition was inaugurated at the Chicago Institute of Art. This was to gather funds in benefit of refugee intellectuals according to Picasso's suggestion. But one cannot say that the result was highly positive. Juan Larrea was given no more than 700 dollars —about 40,000 pesetas—. Picasso had hoped to obtain 10,000 dollars for the Committee for Spanish Culture of the Republican Government. At first sight, the results seem some what disappointing: there were only 735 visitors of 240 dollars. In San Francisco, 535 dollars were obtained. In Chicago, 208, in the Museum of Modern Art, New York, 1,700, with only 2,000 visitors who went to see the picture. A proof of the increased prestige of the work with the passing of time is the fact that in one single day it had 4,000 visitors at its present installations in the Casón. However, reality would have been different had the work enjoyed a raving success then. Only with time does the work which genially surpasses cultural cliché become a common treasure, part of the collective sensibility and intellect. In virtue of the circumstances of the Second World War, Picasso agreed to leave **Guernica** and its sketches in the custody of the Museum of Modern Art in New York. This latter and the painter moved it about the United States, rather more than reasonable if one considers its dimensions and the care and risks involved in its transportation. It went again to Chicago in January 1940; in the summers of 1941 and 1942 it was shown in the Foggs Museum, Harvard. It also crossed the Atlantic and between 1955 and 1956 was exhibited in Cologne, Paris, Hamburg, Munich, Stockholm, Brussels and Amsterdam. The history of these exhibitions should be completed with the data given in the biography of Picasso supplied here and which «Art News» of May 1980 also studied and discussed in an article by that exemplary American Herschel B. Chipp, Professor of the History of Art at Berkeley University, and also in «Guernica —the Picasso Legacy» of October 1981—. With admiring quixotism, Chipp claims in the «New York Times» of the 26th November 1975 that «the hour of **Guernica's** repatriation had come». In the same paper of 1st December 1975, William Rubin, the Director of Painting and Sculpture of the New York Museum of Modern Art, replied hurriedly to this in the sense that **Guernica** could only be given back to Spain when «an authentic Spanish Republic» was reinstalled there, denying other phenomena by the way. This meant that in February 1976[7], it had to be publicly and documentally proved that *in Spain* even Franco had said «yes» to *Guernica* —see the following chapter—. Among the arguments alleged by Rubin in favour of keeping the work in New York, there was that the effect that «Phalangist gangs had raided an exhibition of Picasso's engravings, forgetting that a year bebore —in 1964— a certain Tony Shafrazi had thrown red

---

[7] I had to do this in «Blanco y Negro» (no. 3.328), making the basic facts known.

37   *Third differentiated version of the mother with the dead child*

paint over the work in question in the same
museum of which Rubin was one of the keepers,
and had written in letters of thirty centimetres «Kill
all lies». One could only expect that negotiations
to bring **Guernica** to Spain would fail. The talks
were begun in December 1968, continued in the
following year, and not far into 1970 were wasted
by home-negotiations and strangers alike and
finally, as was to be foreseen, were not accepted
by Picasso. However, as Chipp himself points out,
this negotiation finally «probably caused Picasso to
make his intentions public in 1971», giving clear
instructions to his lawyer, Roland Dumas and
including his intent of donating the sixty-two

9th head of a suffering woman **41**

preparatory works of his own property to Spain. This was the most important point, the most immediately attainable one. Even so, it appears that even in 1972 there was one more attempt to obtain the long-awaited Spanish painting. The only thing left to do was for the Spanish Cortes of 1977 to claim legitimate ownership of same. Even in this way they knew that the arrival of the painting could not be brought about from one day to the next.

At last, not only is **Guernica** in the capital of Spain, but in one of the buildings of the Prado Museum which belongs to all and which is universal. On the morning of the 10th September

1981, it arrived at the regal Casón del Buen Retiro and its public inauguration was held on the 25th October, the commemorative date of the first centenary of its genial painter's birth.

«The Dream and Lie of Franco»

None of those who so tenaciously and brilliantly wrote on *Guernica:* 1. It had to be done in «Blanco y Negro» No. 3,328, giving the most fundamental data. Larrea, Arnheim, Ferrier, Palau i Fabre, were able to omit reference to the two plates for etchings and acquatint of *The Dream and Lie of Franco*. Picasso wrote the title thus in his own handwriting on the cover to the folder for them, and *not* «Songe et mensonge...» in French. This is similar to the way in which he autographed a poetical text in his own native language, just as it is reproduced here, without capital letters, full-stops or commas, doubtless a surrealist poem and in which nothing is intelligible as a political man-ifesto or clear *account* of the Spanish Civil War which motivated it, but which is a pure and simple attempt at verbal creation: «fandango de lechuza escabeche de espadas de pulpos de mal agüero / estropajo de pelos de coronillas de pie en medio de la sartén / en pelotas — puesto sobre el cucurucho del sorbete de bacalao / frito en la sarna de su corazón de cabestro — la boca llena de / la jalea de chinches de sus palabras — cascabeles del plato / de caracoles trenzando tripas — meñique en erección ni uva / ni breva — comedia del arte de mal tejer y teñir nubes / — productos de belleza del carro de la basura —

rapto de las meninas / en lágrimas y en lagrimones
— al hombro del ataúd relleno de chorizos / y de
bocas — la rabia retorciendo el dibujo de la
sombra / que la azota los / dientes clavados en la
arena y el caballo abierto de par en par / al sol que
lo lee a las moscas que hilvanan a los nudos de la /
red llena de boquerones el cohete de azucenas —
farol de piojos / donde está el perro nudo lleno de
ratas y escondrijo del palacio de trapos / viejos —
las banderas que fríen en la sartén se retuercen en
el negro / de salsa de la tinta derramada en las
gotas de sangre que le fusilan / — la calle sube a
las nubes atada por los pies al mar de cera que
pudre / sus entrañas y el velo que la cubre canta y
baila loco de pena — el vuelo / de cañas de pescar
y alhiguí, alhiguí del entierro de primera del carro
de / — mudanza / las alas rotas rodando sobre la
tela de araña del pan seco y / agua clara de la
paella de azúcar y terciopelo que pinta el latigazo
en / sus mejillas — la luz se tapa los ojos delante
del espejo que hace / el mono y el trozo de turrón
de las llamas se muerde los labios / de la herida —
gritos de niños gritos de mujeres gritos de pájaros /
gritos de flores gritos de maderas y de piedras
gritos de ladrillos gritos de / muebles de camas de
sillas de cazuelas de gatos y de papeles / gritos de
olores que se arañan gritos de humo picando en el
morrillo / de los gritos que cuecen el caldero y de
la lluvia de pájaros / que inunda el mar que roe el
hueso y se rompe los dientes / mordiendo el
algodón que el sol rebaña en el plato / que el
bolsón y la bolsa esconden en la huella que el pie /
deja en la roca.»

The first of the two plates bears the date of «8th
January 1937», the second «9th January-7th June»

of the same year. It may easily be assumed that the former was made at one go in a single day. The other was perhaps started on the same day but was probably not finished until several months later (see below), five days after the installation of **Guernica.** At the request of José Gaos, the Spanish commissar at the International Exhibition in Paris, Picasso had agreed to make several etchings of post-card size to be sold at the exhibition itself at a low price and in favour of the Republican cause. Picasso preferred the dimensions 0,31 × 0,42 m and the system of the old popular religious prints with three strips on each card and three drawings or squares on each strip. He set to work on them without paying the slightest attention to the fact that, once they had been printed on the screw press, the handwritten dates and succession of scenes would have to be *read* the wrong way round or the opposite way to western reading systems, that is from right to left. This would have been easy to avoid and has been observed by his commentators. Not few of these later have described them, without raising discussions such as those provoked by interpretations of **Guernica.** Except for one case and certain aspects of another, Franco is portrayed as somewhat absurd, as a grotesque homunculus with a head like a gesticulating and tuberous sweet potato, with a laugh or smile as sly as a vixen's, his teeth clenched, elephantine vermiformoids for eyes and nose and three sphincters with periscopic and undulating finishing touches, a flourishing moustache —either forgotten by the artist or lost by the bearer face-to-face with a bull's head. This head crowned with Mussulmanic head-dresses and other regalia which

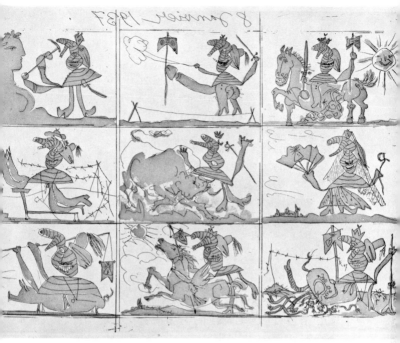

The Dream and Lie of Franco (I)

Franco never wore over his shoulders   for he hadn't got any and, like one who has taken «the world for his own or does not care what anyone would think, as the Spanish saying goes, on a sack which is half the world (part of the world already split in two after the Spanish Civil War?) and which, although it lacks the meridians does have the parallels belonging to it, with arms which stick out of the hemispherical sack, genitals which are on occasion acromegalius and on others barely sufficient. The sequence of «his» *Dream and Lie* is as follows:

The Dream and Lie of Franco (II)

Print I:

1) The sun (topically Spanish?) laughs sarcastically to see how the homunculus rides on a bent old nag that laughs sardonically and from which the whole pack of entrails is dropping out. He weilds a sword in his right hand, whilst in the same hand he brandishes a frying-pan by the handle (the one in the popular saying?), hoisting in his left a pennant with a devout Marian image the crown of which is finished in the half-moon of the Moorish troops with which he began his well-known war campaign.

Guernica (Detail)

2) With a huge Moorish head-dress and little crown, a determined tightrope-walker, the freak crosses a wide space —clearly the Straits of Gibraltar— letting himself be transported by a cloud with the wind in his favour, tied by ropes on one of his hands, the sword in the other, with huge testicles —again a theme common in Spanish colloquial language— pushing the pennant with a Priapic and colossal phallus, the pennant here with two circles —spheres?-worlds?— separated by a triangle.

3) With his sword on the sack, mitred and with a half-mooned turban, the aggressive monster,

with the two hands —«balls»— of its phallic arms, weilds a pickaxe with which it is about to destroy a great solemn and beautiful female bust, with a classical profile and light garland round its head and, down from its opulent beasts, is inseparably united with the earth; this bust must be Spain, or any other elevated concept and, had the Republic so wished it to be, it would have cost no effort to crown it with the corresponding mural. (Note the *coincidence* of this strip with Goya's impressive drawing which is so rightly called *He does not know what he is doing* of a blind ruffian on a hand-ladder, who has smashed a beautiful female bust with a pickaxe. One should also remember, with regard to this type of furious iconoclast, what is written below on the broken male statue in **Guernica.**

4) Jocular and sprightly, the freak swaggers in a transparent skirt under the semispherical sack, a fan with the Virgin in its right hand, a mantilla hanging from a high comb with a microscopic half-moon, a twisted sabre in its hand and a distant town in which one would have to strain one's eyes to see the Giralda and Tower of Gold of Seville —*topical* Spain, as against *real-ideal* Spain which we had previously seen demolished?

5) The sword flies into the air with the crown and frightening half-moon, which does not laugh now at the charge of the noble, aggressive bull—doubtless the mythically «Iberian» one, to judge from the symbology of **Guernica.**

6) Quite probably, on account of the previous charge, the little monster has no other alternative but to implore the higher spheres, finding itself enclosed in thorny barbed wire, its genitality all

lost when in the second strip it had made so much show of it kneeling on a prie-dieu with a double, or maybe triple, Moorish head-dress, praying to a monstrance on the inner monstrance of which one can clearly read inverted «1 DURO», for as Quevedo tells us «Poderoso caballero es Don Dinero» (Mr. Money is a powerful gent.).

7) Perhaps because the money had been already obtained, the barbed wire knocked down, with a half-moon crown and the already much seen Northafrican head-dress, one of his vermiform eyes pointed and without a sphincter, this is why the freak has stuck its pennant of Marian devotion into the udder on which it is seated or is kicking and through the vulva of which one can see public hair and well-opened vaginal lips bearing forth toads and serpents (Did Picasso know Ortega y Gasset's prophetic essay on the udders of the *Dwarf Gregory the Bootmaker* —in the Moscow Museum— by Ignacio Zuloaga?). Thus the freak, while it holds in its right hand masculine genitals which are vertically erect from the ground and held by a cord (?) —and one knows how, in anger, envy or hate, with strong language, one says in Spain that one must tear them off of this, that or the other.

8) Having venged his thirst for prey, and with the same head-dress as before, the phoetus attempts to gallop on or knock over a winged Pegasus, a noble horse and no old nag such as that in the first strip, which observes a darkening sun surrounded by light clouds, pierced by the oftmentioned pennant through one of its flanks, all its four legs in the air against a background in which

one can see a village or a ruin, barbed wire or a broken-down peasant fence.

9) As Pegasus was only worthy of aggression, the homunculus prefers to ride upon a flagging, seedy pig, whilst he brandishes the miracle-performing pennant in both hands, threatening another sun which seems to be afraid of him or to be retreating.

Print II:

10) Having stuck the pennant in the earth, and having dressed itself in a half-moon mitre and Islamic fez, the homunculus once again attacks Pegasus and strives to tear off one of its wings once the horse has been overthrown on the ground and is writhing in agory.

11) It is not known why, but suddenly the deformed nightmare of the homunculus disappears from the scene and a young and beautiful woman lies on the landscape; she is luminous, her wide-open eyes staring at the sky without any trace of terror or suffering (placidly dead?), or perhaps she is there to remind the spectator of Machado's verses: «¿Espera, duerme o sueña? ¿La sangre derramada / recuerda, cuando tuvo la fiebre de la espalda?» (Does he wait, sleep or dream? Does the bloodshed bring back memories of when he had the fever of the sword?)

12) A man and a horse also lie on the ground in a mutual embrace which does not seem lacking in tenderness. The eyes of the man are similar to those of the beautiful woman.

13) A close-up of a tuberous and even more repulsive hairy head, for the first time with open toothless jaws, with the crown and its half-moon like a staggering top on the upper part of the hemispherical sack which, now even more clearly than ever —and like the work—, spins dizzily bringing the monster face-to-face with the radiant and unrivalled head of an «Iberian» bull, the same as the next one, both of which should be taken into account in considering **Guernica.** (Could we once more see in this, as we did in the former example, faced with this square and the pierced horse and the male statue of *Guernica,* other verses by Machado when he complained: *«Españolito que vienes / al mundo, te guarde Dios. / Una de las dos Españas / ha de helarte el corazón.»* (God keep you, little Spaniard, who come into the world. For one of the two Spains is bound to freeze your heart»).

14) The powerful bull, now enraged, has opened up a gash in the freak, which is here metamorphosed into a four-legged horse-like beast (the fact should be borne in mind as regards the horse in the large canvas), which shows its anus splayed wide without male genitals, all its entrails spilling forth, a jumbled mess of innards in which the sabre, flag and pennant are to be seen, its head even more elephantine and swinish than ever on a long, robust vermiform neck that it had never had before, its mouth wide open on account of the painful spasm caused by the ferocious attack.

(From the previous square onwards, we are faced with the following variants which should be noted: Picasso stops using acquatint; he uses an even more sweeping style of drawing which contrasts above all with that of the two former strips, which are precisely the most elaborate of all, so that one may reach the conclusion that the first five of this print were done some time before (on the 8th and 9th January 1937 and the remaining and final ones from the 7th June of the same year?); the drawing has at least in two cases a close relationship to a good deal of the so-called «preparatory» works for **Guernica,** few of which were in fact transcribed in the work; the irascible freak disappears for good for, after the horror of Guernica and the turn the war is taking, couldn't one take him as a joke? the old concern which, together with his daughter Maya, Picasso had cultivated in order that his hand and brain should truly draw like those of a child is seen to be *in crescendo* in the three final squares.)

15) Tragedy is irresistible: her arms raised, a female profile —that of many versions of the drawings for **Guernica** sends a blood-curdling cry to the air— praying? imploring? The devouring flames also blaze upwards in the background.

16) Another woman, the one in other diverse, so-called «preparatory» drawings, who was to figure differently in the large work, shouts out like the former and, like someone who has to drag himself under the burder of his sorrow, bares her maternal and symbolic breast, carrying her dead child in her arms as she flees from her burned-out home. Is the scratch engraved in the hills to the left a tree or the explosion of a bomb?

17) In the foreground, the horror has left the faces of the mother and child, for both lie dead (cf. what may be coincidences: could both be related as far as the idea and not their portrayal is

Guernica
Canvas, oil-paint 350 × 780 cm

concerned with the third canvas of the triptych by Arteta mentioned above?).

18) Horror and screams are unbridled in this final jumble of lines and characters, drawn in a completely «childish» style. An arrow (one of those of the bellicose Phalange?) has pierced the woman's neck, whilst her face is turned in profile to the sky. Two children hug her terrified. The corpse of a man lies dead and crosses the composition from side to side. Are the mountains in the landscape smoking from bombing raids?

At least at the end of the *Caprices* Goya was to

leave a loophole for hope. It seems that in 1937, two years before the end of the Spanish Civil War and the beginning of the Second Workd War, Picasso could not find one for his *Dream and Lie of Franco,* although perhaps he was to find it in **Guernica.**

Not merely through the type of common jokes or anecdotes such as circulated round Spain for forty years do I know from totally trustworthy sources that on a certain occasion —almost thirty years ago— two personalities of the world of art had to visit Franco, and on the way to El Pardo decided firmly not to mention Picasso's name on any account whilst they were talking to Franco. But it was Franco himself who brought it into the conversation and who left them quite perplexed when he said that during the war Picasso had made certain engravings —those of the *Dream and Lie*— poking fun at the general and at «us» as was his expression on the occasion and which were indeed «very interesting». Could this have been an equanimous judgement before an artistic creation? Or was it ironic Galician humour? Or was it the olympic and unflinching gaze of the victor? Even before this it was rumoured in Spain that even Franco had said «yes» to bringing **Guernica** to Spain. The logical thing, however, was that Picasso should then have said «no».

An engraving of 1935: «Minotauromachy» plus other works of the same chronological environment

It would be rare for anybody who, upon discussing **Guernica,** its meanings and genesis, did not bring into the matter the etching which Picasso did in 1935 with the title, which is as clear as it is unclarifying, of *Minotauromachy*[8]. Most critics, when they think of **Guernica,** base their arguments on this print among other things to try to verify who are the «goodies» and who are the «baddies» of the huge work: whether Minos-toro, the bull or the horse, which positive or negative symbolic values one or another might have, as likewise the

---

[8] In 1982, the Ministry of Culture obtained a print of this important etching, to exhibit it with the other works by Picasso in the Casón.

rest of the figures, in the artist's mind and in the result of his work. They do well in this, although the *Minotauromachy* is no more nor less than the enigmatic puzzle of a dream, an apotheosic string of oneiric images and as such it is intricately biographical. That is, in Hispano-Goyesque terms: «caprice» ludic creativity, «invention» —discovery— and «widening» or opening up the path of wher- ever the creator might wish to go. Goya would have called it the «Folly of Minos», «Folly of the little girl»... or perhaps, also, «neither sleep nor the candle keep the monster away». In this way, rather than with its apparently precise title of *Mino- tauromachy*, we would have been obliged to pay more attention, our disconcertment still hyper- tensed, and would have been forced to penetrate right through to the marrow of such a highly ordered and disconcerting oneiric marquetry.

The man who keeps a safe distance climbing the ladder to look at Minos, happens to closely re- semble the young men who run in front of the bulls in Spain and who climb up wherever they can to watch them pass. The girl with the little light (could it be the still youthful Marie Thérèse who was to give birth to Maya in 1935?) who in a serenely contemplative way lights up and watches the great Mediterranean beast could mean that Picasso himself did not wish to see this type of illumination with his own eyes. The old, valetud- inarian equine raptor (could it be the by now unappetising Olga?) looks at the Minotaur with hate and neighs insultingly. In such a way, the mare —or nag— still under the sword of the woman bull-fighter on top of her, lies sleeping and in her rape, death or sleep wishes to frighten her off

or eliminate her. A beautiful female with the naked bosom of the charming female bull-jumpers of the ancient bull-ring at Cnossos, the Cretean art, sport, dance and rite of danger. The stormy cloud which pours its torrential rain into the swollen sea. And lastly, the two young women at the window who only pay attention to the pair of doves which eat or drink in the bowl and which perhaps coo peacefully and dreamily, far removed from any drama great or small.

Four elements may be considered to be related in this engraving to another four which are related to *Guernica:*

The man on the ladder, who resembles two «preparatory» drawings with a frightened woman with her dead child in her arms; the girl with the candle, in a way comparable to the overwhelming woman with the lamp, and by the way with a bouquet of flowers as if for a wedding that could never be, if, in fact, this was Marie Thérèse. The Minotaur with its good-natured face, a Cretan bull and also a reminder of the Iberian one. And the ugly horse which nothing in its gestures and form makes pleasant and which therefore, on thinking of the other in **Guernica,** one might assume to be a transferable symbol of those who were the «enemy» to Picasso or any other repudiated reality.

The day Juan Larrea had the idea of asserting that the horse in **Guernica** represented Franquism unleashed a huge polemical discussion and one in fact which is still unfinished. In this, Anglo-Saxon critics tried their utmost to contradict Larrea, to the point of haughty contempt, whilst Picasso just shrugged his shoulders and refused to pass any comments. Like one who did not wish to stir up any more trouble, he refused to specify the symbols he had in fact placed in his painting. This was doubtless on account of some deep reason that, although he had engendered **Guernica,** this latter had to explain itself away. For, once it had left his hands, it was a creature with its own life and was even independent of him. This is the most any great creator can aspire to: that the offspring of his mind, as likewise the children of his flesh, take care of themselves and free themselves as soon as possible from the smothering paternalism and logomachic vigilance of each parent.

In the same way as there is no man capable of explaining another man completely, the enigma of intimate and alien humanity, if it is not by means of a cordial although perplexed approach, great works such as **Guernica** cannot refer to the spectator without a fertile sensation of constant doubt, which is far removed from any dogmatism and with the knowledge that fortunately, they are a permanent problem in which we are all incited in a myriad different ways, to participate, both with a logical and attentive examination as regards the visibly concrete and with the sensitive irrationality with which we are endowed from birth to death and which it would be a disastrous castration not to exercise.

Picasso came to say of the bull that it was «brutality and obscurity», but it is frequently supposed and asserted that the one in **Guernica** and a good many of his other bulls are «self-portraits» of the artist, on account of the autobiographical nature which has also been pointed out in his vast output. Which is less contradictory and paradoxical than it would seem at first. This would

perhaps seem less contradictory and paradoxical than may be thought at first glance. For the bull, like Picasso, may be understood to be an overwhelming mental force with which to face up to existence, as against the brutality and blindness of a technologically trained human species which is ready for all sorts of the so-called «bestialities». This is similar to the way in which those who believe that we can perceive in the horse black and hidden depths, perhaps masked by its fine image and even more so by its condition of human domestic animal, or lordly «noble» beast.

It is said that the horse made man a rider, but the truth is that only a very few of countless others were made in this way, by means of the horse and the ennobling possession of same which was not within the range of just any mortal. The Spanish people were the pawns, commoners, infantrymen, squires for centuries and centuries of wars, to such an extent that they rode either asses or mules and if they got any higher than this, then no higher than Sancho on Rucio. This is for the same reason that Don Quixote, the alienated wandering knight to be de-mythified, rode on a nag, on a poor, worthless beast of burden, an animal wearied by its load, the well-loved Rocinante of all Spaniards, less worthy of the decorum due to an elevated knightly mount. Since time immemorial, mounted knights have lanced bulls in Spain, thus regaling the plebeyan spectators with the image of their *unattainable* nobility. Even the pawn, the «chulo» —thus they were to call him— who served the grandees on foot, took over the bull-fight and subverted the horse into the picador. And the power of the bull and the courage of the bull-

113

fighter which were to be measured against him were to be seen in the number of miserable nags which left the villainous bull-ring disembowelled. The popular collective sub-conscious smothered the servant of both nobles and people in silver and gold, silks and embroidery. In the midst of multitudinarian amazement, he was made absolute master of the ring: «sword», «deft-hand», «master», on the shoulders of his own triumph and collective revenge. At the same time the less graceful side of each bloody and resplendent fight was brought about: that of the rough, graceless task of the picador —note that he is never called «lancer»— who time and again was to bear the bull's charges, charges of the savagely male Iberian country bull. Later there was to be compassion for the horses. This was perhaps because hundreds and hundreds of riders were seen to be *somehow sacrificed* together with them, ritually and in the innermost corner of the common herd's soul. Not for this reason was the participant in the bull-fight the one who aroused the greatest fury and booing. After all, nobody would say that the fine art of fighting, lancing and killing bulls on horseback was precisely essential to the so-called Spanish «national fiesta».

Picasso's *Minotauromachy* of 1935 focusses attention on the spin-chilling group of the beautiful and almost naked female bullfighter stretched across the repulsive nag which both hates and curses the virile man-bull. It should moreover be borne in mind that Goya had already dealt with the theme in one of his oneiric *Follies*. In the first place he did a preliminary drawing in which a fine horse kidnaps a horrified girl, a male figure lying kicked to death behind them. Later, he did a final etching of the same in which the woman is seen to be laughing and enjoying the rape of the frenzied horse against a background of hallucinatory hills like gigantic beasts of prey, or immense freaks which have come to light from heaven knows what caverns or unknown sewers. One of them has open jaws so that another woman may walk in on her own feet to be devoured without any violence. There is no doubt that in each case Goya's dream was different. The first point is perhaps that taken by Goya when he was really asleep, and the following one whilst he was kept awake so that he was able to penetrate further into the mysteries of black human subconsciousness. The first of these points is the most important with regard to the horse of **Guernica.** In it, Goya's «noble» (at least formally) horse has kicked the man to death, not only taking his life but also his companion, there being not the slightest doubt that the dead man was not precisely of knightly origin, but of the common people alone. In the human subconscious, the horse is the raptor. It kills and rapes. And this has to be said thus, although certain repulsive aesthetic conventions must be overcome, for one cannot help looking at the horse in quite a different way, even with the Phydian beauty of those of Helios, Selena or the Parthenon. We should not now turn our attention to history, which is studded with such noble and aristrocratic riders, but to intrahistorical experience as lived and made by a multitude of enslaved men who were oppressed by those who swaggered on horseback, on the fine noble beast which those who were deprived of such luck came to regard unconsciously as a fierce brute and an incriminat-

2 *A second sketch and the first approach to symbological lucubration*

ing image of subjugating power, in a similar way to that in which Goya's brilliant intuition shows us.

It is not difficult to find examples of the theme of rape in Picasso's work. They come in the guise of similar species to those of his *Minotauromachy* and those of Goya's drawings and engravings which we mentioned above. In a highly beautiful etching of 1934, the bull and a beautiful naked female bullfighter kiss each other; she is lying across the disembowelled nag which has died an «ignoble death». Contrarily, because creative equivocity functions like this in art, it is a pierced bull that carries a horse with a naked, kidnapped female bullfighter in an oil painting kept in the

116

Picasso Museum in Paris —Zervos, VIII, 138, of 1933. This resembles another painting in the same museum— Zervos VIII 214, of 1933, in which as in many other instances in this and other epochs of Picasso's, the neighing head of the horse bears a strong resemblance to that of **Guernica** and several others of his «preparatory» studies. The same may perhaps help to clarify the antagonical symbology of the horse and the bull in the *Guernica* as in an ink and gouache drawing —Zervos VIII, 388 of 1936 in the Picasso Museum, Paris— in which Pegasus, in this case malign and with flaming wings, brutally kicks the Minotaur which lies pierced on the ground. This may thus be related to the statue of a warrior in **Guernica.** Although in a

Five graphic-emotional automatisms **3**

different context, another drawing may have a similar meaning; it is done in the same technique and year —also in the Picasso Museum, Paris— in which the Minotaur bears the dead vanquished horse in its Herculean arms, having snatched it from a cave from which hands emerge imploringly, whilst the left side of the mythical bull-man is thrust forward in a similar way to the right side of it in the *Minotauromachy* engraving, as though retreating from the delicate woman's figure which appears at the very right of the background. A true image of the horse being dragged to death is that of a drawing —Zervos, IX, 83— of a horse which resists being dragged to the fight by a groom —the picador's mate—. This drawing is believed to be on a circus theme, when there is no doubt at all that is refers to the world of bull-fighting. Perhaps the most terrible example of the antagonism between bull and horse is that displayed in another drawing —Zervos VIII, 215, Picasso Museum, Paris of 1934— in which the lanced bull vomits its blood over the entrails of the horse which have been spilled by goring. In addition to this a young woman appears in the gory scene and looks on, shading her eyes from the light of the candle held in her other hand. This is a clear forerunner of the girl in the *Minotauromachy* and the woman with the lamp in **Guernica** We shall quote one final drawing of those that could be quoted in this context —Zervos VIII, 276, Picasso Museum, Paris of the 5th April, 1936— which proves that in the sphere of Picasso's mind it was not easy, for the bull —or man-bull— and the horse could be alive, well and at peace with each other together. In this drawing, the Minotaur overthrows the cart which bears the corpse of a mare in whose gored belly one can see the foal she was carrying.

The foregoing has been written with the constant doubt that, despite the examples and reasons given, the horse of **Guernica** may also be interpreted as one more *victim* of the disaster, which is explained below. We could hardly penetrate the heights of human artistic creation if we forgot that in many instances there operates a constantly polyvalent equivocity, the multiplication of possible points of view and interpretations, and the attitude towards it as a problem in which all may intervene in search of a personal «solution» with which one feels psychically and experientially moved, thus enriching both spectators and participants.

On the «preparation» and process of «Guernica»

Certain critics have not omitted to quote certain declarations by the artist, with regard to **Guernica** and others of his works, in which it may be said by the way, there would be nothing absurd at all should they appear contradictory. Two years after painting the great work for the Spanish pavillion of the Paris Exhibition of 1937, Picasso expresses himself thus:

«It would be most interesting to preserve photographically not the stages but the metamorphoses of a painting. Possibly one would thus be able to discover the path followed by the brain to materialize a *dream*. But there is something very strange and that is to observe that a painting does

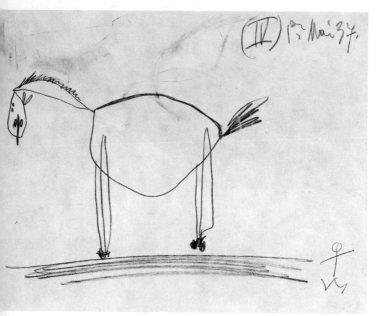

4   *An even more «childish» horse*

not basically change, that the first *vision* remains almost *intact,* despite appearances.»

The foregoing is a presupposition which would drive the logistics of more than one art historian mad with joy but which was soon afterwards to be thwarted to a great extent by Picasso when he made a statement which seems to contradict the above:

«A painting is not thought out and decided beforehand. Whilst it is in the making, it changes as each of our thoughts may change.»

Picasso complicates this, and one might have expected him to do so, when he adds:

«In ancient times, paintings were given their finishing touches in stages. Each day brought

Two attempts for another horse **5**

something new. A painting used to be the sum of
actions. In my case, a painting is the sum of
destructions. I paint a work, and then I destroy it.»

This *at least* means that Picasso was able to work
with the three mechanisms of the creative in
tellect: the basis of the *dream-vision,* which would
come first and would reach the end *almost* un-
touched, although the thought would often
change, and finally, destruction. Of these three
types of intellectual activity, the first and third are
valid for **Guernica** in themselves, for the initial
sketch —the ensemble of its evanescent totality—
reaches the goal almost fully that is, once it has
attained its fullness, whilst in the process of work,
the work underwent the partial mutations or

destructions which the seven —or rather eight— photos preserved of its process reveal. The changes are of such magnitude that they doubtless required a good deal of courage to carry out. And the second may be applied to the tangled «preparatory» studies in the diverse images and ideas which often change and which were only in small measure made to function in the final work. Let no-one think by this that Picasso wasted time, but quite the opposite.

His attitude was to be quite different towards the trouble caused by those who were involved in polemics or by interviewers, the odd-jobbers of a journalism which does not pay royalties for intellectual property offered by the well-exploited grey matter of those assaulted by their interviews. These latter are often dispatched without the slightest rigour and they make themselves look clever through the intelligence of others. In this way, Picasso, weary of questions, and more than once going off at a tangent, was to state, if he did in fact pronounce it thus, that:

«This bull is a bull, this horse is a horse. There is also a sort of bird, a chicken or pigeon, I can't remember which, on the table. This chicken is a chicken. Yes, of course, the *symbols... But the painter does not need to create those symbols.* Otherwise, it would be better to write once and for all what one wants to write instead of painting it. *The public, the spectators, must see in the horse or in the bull symbols* (then the painter *had* created them!) *which they should interpret as they wish...* That is, «let the public see what it wants».

And this is what we, the «public» at the service of others, are trying to do. And this is what we shall continue to do in the following pages on the «preparatory» works, the seven —eight— photos taken by Dora Maar of the different stages of the work and the work itself.

The «Preparatory» studies

The first thing which should be said about them is that they represent three clearly defined types, genres or species: the very few which were in fact done prior to the great canvas; those which were simultaneous with it; and those carried out *a posteriori*. That is, it is impossible to consider them all as «preparatory» or as though they were a sort of hangover for a prolonged period from the tension created by the emotion that seized Picasso and which he was to portray with no little effort. In view of the fact that many of them were not used nor even designed to be used in the final version of **Guernica,** one may take as valid the hypothesis that they came from Picasso's hands with the pyscho-graphic automatism of one who scribbles down his mental flux whilst he attends to higher matters. In the case of Picasso this meant being lucidly attentive to the intellectual problem in which he was involved in order to solve the final work both dialectically and pictorially. He was like one who attends a great conclave of judgements, opinions and suppositions, whilst intoxicated by the fundamental theme and one who thus makes a few scrawls on paper instead of taking written notes. On the importance of such *surrealist* auto-matism, it should not be forgotten that in the months prior to **Guernica** Picasso had been doing just this with whatever it came to him to write and which in fact had functioned in the now transcribed text (for these and other reasons) of the *Dream and Lie of Franco,* a literary offspring which made no effort to verbally explain the consecutive 18 strips which it «prolonged».

These are the prior, parallel and *a posteriori* works to **Guernica.** It has been observed that a great many of them were done successively on three types of paper: intense blue, slightly warm white and leaves from an album of so-called «cloth-paper»:

1. *The germinal sketch for* **Guernica.** Deep blue paper, graphite, 0,209 × 0,269. Autographed in French: *(I) 1st May 37:* of a minimally horizontal format despite the lengthy proportions the «mural» was to take on. It is a very quick sketch in which the bull (lanced? with Pegasus on top of it?) to the left may be seen, as likewise a chaotic mass in the centre which is still uninterpretable, and the shape of the lamp thrown over this latter from a window, plus an almost complete circumference which surrounds a good part of the central vaguely amorphous mass. It could quite well be the jotting down of the elliptic dynamics which were finally to function in the composition of **Guernica** and which lies hidden in the tangle of its triangular and other rectilinear structures. Although so nebulous and imprecise, this is probably the only preparatory work which deserves the name of «sketch». The others of its type are in the guise of parallel approaches to the theme planned and in which its content and symbols could be lucubrated by giving free rein to the energy unleashed in the

artist's mind by the hypertense conception of the great paiting.

2. *A Second sketch and the first approach to symbological lucubration.* Deep blue paper, graphite, 0,21 × 0,27. Autographed in French: *(II) 1st May 37.* Separated by a horizontal line, with an accurate eye for the length which the final work was to have. A) A highly summary sketch, vaguer and quicker than the former; the body of the bull and its head are turned to the centre, this latter left to be filled in with a few pencil traces; on the left there is the house and a vague indication that the figure with the lamp will prevail, whilst even further to the right there are a few vertical strokes which may be considered as a compositional anticipation of the door which figures in the final work. B) Below the former; surely concerned with elaborating the *symbology* of the theme which was churning in the artist's mind; the horse as foreseen, was brutally deformed and mortally wounded, its neck erect and its large skull neighing in pain, but to the left of the sketch; the bull, truly noble and handsome, takes up the centre and to culminate it, with its excessive, candorous and shameless symbolism rides or floats on the small, winged Pegasus; to the right, there is no more than the insinuation of another quadruped, certainly a horse, kneeling on the ground with elegant forelegs and the neck begun as a prolongation of its beautiful, curved line to the unfinished haunches.

3. *Five graphic-emotional automatisms.* Deep blue paper, graphite, 0,21 × 0,268. Autographed in French. *(III) 1st May 37.* 1) The horse on the left of the previous drawing, with an open window in its lemon-shaped belly through which something

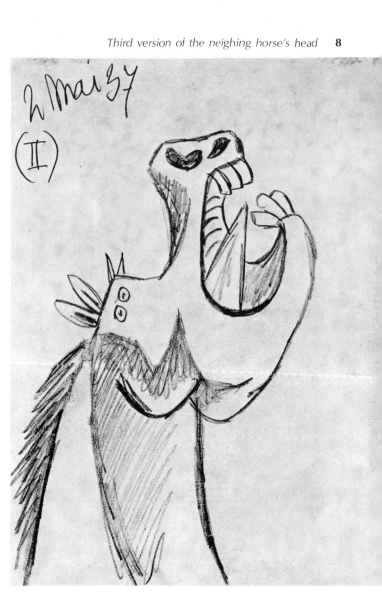

must have escaped and which was to be erased and placed where the horse's head is 3). 2) The persistent image of the woman with the lamp, although here she brandishes a far too «bourgeoise» table-lamp. 3) The horse neighing and defeated, skull downwards, immense neck and the body of an insolent kicking arachnid. 4) A woman gored open with her entrails spilling forth, with a horizontal ellipse which perhaps heightens the «childish» nature of the work —and to this effect, the most successful— in its ensemble, or which maybe suggests that the figure should be placed lying down and not in vertical position, its head being the first glimpse of what was to be a long series of supine women. 4) Vertically framed, although to be viewed horizontally —thus it is explained by the word «bas» at the bottom— a long-necked horse is to be seen, its head turned upwards, with a pear-shaped body and short, knock-kneed legs, which is magnificently «childish». With regard to these strange anatomic forms of Picasso's which are *articulated* together by the mere, highly reduced contact of one with another, one should remember, for example, the drawing *Couple making love* of 1933 —Zervos, VIII, 107, Picasso Museum, Paris.

4. *An even more «childish» horse*. Deep blue paper, graphite, 0,21 × 0,27. Autographed in French: *(IV) 1st May 37. Signed (?)...* in the bottom right-hand corner *with a doodle:* head = circumference; body = vertical line; arms = cross-line; legs and feet = a W which finishes off the vertical line. (It has often been repeated how Picasso stated it had cost him great pains to manage to draw like a child.) This was doubtless done with liberating

automatism, carried out whilst other turbulent forms and «adult» creative preoccupations teemed in his brain. It was as if he said: How easily children express the formal reality of a horse!...

5. *Two attempts for another horse.* Deep blue paper, graphite, 0,21 × 0,267. Autographed in French: *(V) 1st May 37.* A) Strokes with slight pressure from the pencil and rubbed out where the head of this unfinished horse should have been. B) Drawn over the former. Rather more of a *verist* version of the ill-treated horse, which lies on the ground neighing upwards to the sky. (See 20.)

6. *The second approach to a general symbological lucubration.* Canvas with a first layer of stained white oil-paint, graphite 0,536 × 0,649. Autographed in French: *1st May 37,* the last to be done on this date. The artist's rectifications are clearly seen. The bull looks to the left and takes up the centre with its hind quarters, its tail reaching almost to the right-hand margin of the total framework. Notably male from behind although no so much so by its head which is crowned with a graceful, womanly garland. One can see a Pegasus above it which the artist has erased, covering it with the oil-paint used here. Lying from side to side (see strip 16 of the *Dream and Lie of Franco*) the dead warrior appears, with an old helmet on his head and the lance with which he must have mortally wounded the neighing horse, here drawn with a pointed tongue (see the following one) and from the belly of which a winged, very small and far too symbolical Pegasus is freed. The head of this horse in pain was to be a motif that Picasso was to study in subsequent works. It neighs and looks towards the woman with the lamp and the

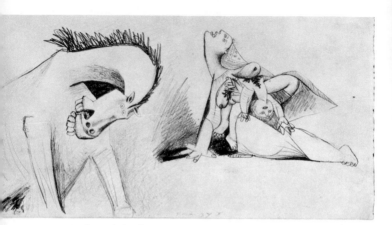

13   *Studies of the horse and mother with dead child for the former attempt*

window that so far have not been displaced. The first layer is of white oil-paint and not stucco, as other American cataloguers have asserted. It helped Picasso to cover up the efforts he realized the work was to cost him.

7.   *Second version of the neighing horse's head of the former drawing.* Deep blue paper, cut irregularly on the right-hand edge, graphite 0,210 × 0,155. Autographed in French: *2nd May 37 (I)*. Picasso went over the drawings of the previous day's work and found that, from the last one onwards, it was worth while doing variations on the same theme: that of the horse with the neighing head and cone-shaped tongue, a tongue which both animals were to have in *Guernica,* as likewise the woman with the dead child. In 1931, the hallucinatory *Figures by the Sea* —Zervos, VII, 328, Picasso Museum, Paris— had already been portrayed with such a tongue and were represented as two dislocated lovers «kissing» each

other with erotic frenzy with their vicious pointed tongues in oneiric and surrealistic copulation. He repeated the horse's head placing the upper teeth over the nose, whilst they had formerly been to one side of same. What did he wish to express most by this: pain or ferociousness?

8. *Third version of the neighing horse's head.* Deep blue paper. Graphite, 0,266 × 0,210. Autographed in French: *2nd May 37 (II)*. The teeth are drawn in an almost natural position.

9. *Fourth, oil-paint version of the neighing*

Third version of the mother with the dead child **14**

horse's head. On canvas, oil-paint, 0,647 × 0,923. Autographed in French: *2nd May 37*. The teeth are painted more or less the same as in the first portrayal of the horse (see 6). There is a black background, the head looking like a grisaille. The eyes have been given a heightened expression of fear.

10. *Third approach to the general lucubration.*

Canvas with several layers of white oil-paint, graphite 0,60 × 0,725. Autographed in French: *2nd May 37*. There are still no forms or references which lead one to think that this is the actual fact of the bombing of Guernica: planes, flames, the town's venerated tree, easily identifiable Basques, swastikas... The horse crushes the warrior with the lance with its now well-known head (the warrior now takes the form of a beheaded statue) as likewise another character whose formal thinness reminds one of the *Crucifixion* (1930) and *The Death of Marat* (1931) in the Picasso Museum, Paris. On top of the pile of corpses, the bull with the human face runs and jumps, looking somewhat crestfallen. The woman with the lamp takes on greater solidity and one can even see four triangular breasts on her like the old, fecund Magna Mater of the East. Is the bull now responsible for the heap of slaughter under him? The expressionist features of the previous works are still to be seen on the horse's head. The various forms of the composition take on greater or lesser whiteness with the several layers of oil-paint.

11. *Once more the problem of the horse and bull*. Brown-coloured card, with cuts at each of the left-hand corners, graphite 0,225 × 0,12. Dateless. Perhaps Picasso is again in doubt: would it be right to define the symbols of «good» and «evil» categorically? Except for the position of its eyes, the long-necked horse's head recovers formal normality and loses the pointed, cone-shaped tongue, seeming somehow humanized without its teeth. On the other hand, the bull —fully portrayed here— is deformed and takes on a malign agressivity with horns in the shape of small half-moons, its nostrils

like a well cared-for moustache and its tongue in the shape of a curved sharp eye-tooth. Both animals are drawn with Picasso's masterful confidence of stroke.

12. *Fourth attempt at a general lucubration*. White paper, graphite, 0,24 × 0,45. Autographed in French: *8th May 37*. The bull is fully placed in the centre and is solemn and quite calm. Its face is even «handsome». Beneath and in front of it, the horse is about to flop onto the dead warrior and holds itself stubbornly up on its stiff forelegs, its eyes and dreadful neigh turned on the placid face of the dead warrior. The woman with the lamp has disappeared, perhaps because Picasso took it for granted that she was to stay there. On the right there is the mother of the dead child, a character which was to go over to the left in the large canvas underneath the huge bull. From this point onwards, Picasso was to find sufficient material to portray her. (See also the end of the *Dream and Lie of Franco*.)

13. *Studies of the horse and mother with dead child for the former attempt:* White paper, graphite, 0,239 × 0,455. Autographed in French: *8th May 37(II)*. A) The former horse is formally perfected and does not fall to the ground. B) A very careful study of the mother and child kneeling with one hand on the ground, her pained profile uplifted, and a large scarf round her formerly shaven head; bloodstained, the dead child seems to spring from between his mother's breasts. These latter are very sensually elaborated.

14. *Third version of the mother with the dead child*. White paper, black ink and pen drawing, 0,24 × 0,45. Autographed in French: *9th May 37 (I)*

(see the two former ones). Done in a far more impetuous style than the previous pencil one, it displays the following variants: one of the child's arms is curled round one of his mother's breasts and her left hand hides a good deal of her other breast, by which the strong emotional impact is somewhat diluted from that produced before in the stiff little arms which hung under the free, uncovered nakedness of the mother's breasts.

15. *Fifth attempt at a general lucubration:* White paper, graphite, 0,24×0,45. Autographed in French: *9th May 37 (II).* To the right the flames appear for the first time. The arrangement of large, dark areas now suggests a night scene. It should be remembered in this context that the raid on Guernica was begun in the evening light. Blocks of houses lie to right and left. The woman with the lamp (see 12) reappears. Beneath her and to her right, an enormous arm with raised fist is coming through a window. The impassive bull takes up almost the centre of the composition. Lying along the groundline, there is an *untidy* heap of corpses, the wheel from a peasant's cart and the fallen horse with the mother and child —this latter still to the right—. To the left, there are the two heads of a man and woman who share a single neck. The geometricised arrangement of the light and dark spaces is of special importance.

16. *The mother with the dead child on a ladder:* White paper, graphite, 0,45×0,24. Autographed in French: *9th May 37 (III).* This bears a certain resemblance to the man on the ladder in the *Minotauromachy* (cf.) of 1935. The corpse of the child is pressed in anguish to the turgid, naked breasts of the mother. Picasso was to paint the

17   *The fallen horse*

theme again in No. 21 with greater concern for the contrasts of light and dark. This is a highly pathetic solution, but was not to be used in the final work.

17.   *The fallen horse:* White paper, graphite, 0,24 × 0,45. Autographed in French: *10th May 37 (I).* Step by step, the horse has fallen to the ground although this was not to be so in the final work. Here it seems to be in its death-throes and is certainly conceived and portrayed as a *victim.* It is drawn with far greater formal freedom, albeit without exaggerating its constructive defor-mations.

18.   *A horse's leg and two horse's heads.* White paper, graphite, 0,45 × 0,24. Autographed in French: 10th May 37 (II). Straight after the previous drawing, Picasso returns to the expressive problem of the neighing horse (see drawings 6-7) (fallen, dying or dead, it could have produced compassion in the spectator). As in the ones we have just discussed, the two heads portrayed here lack the agressively sharp, cone-shaped tongue. However,

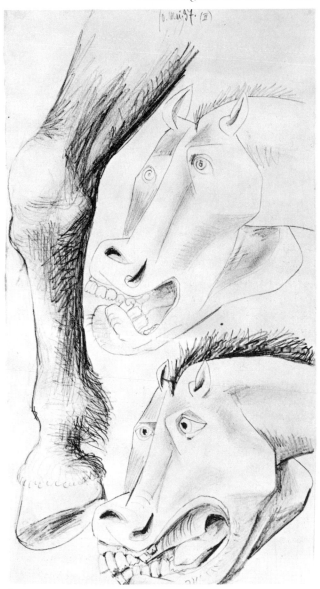

what seems to be the aim in the mouth of one of them is the repetition of the expression of intimidating fury. At the very least, its gesture is not exactly one of pain neither is it comforting. The same happens with its eyes. The leg is drawn with effective verism, and there is no concern with the plastic and creative deformations of the heads.

19. *Head of a deific, androcephalous bull.* White paper, graphite, 0,45 × 0,24. Autographed in French: *10th May 37 (III).* Its face is more Apollonian than Pan-like, and is of godly lucidity, young and serene. Picasso doubtless wished to endow it with the same intelligence as the dark, biological force of the mythical bull, just as had occurred in the impressive religious inconology of the remote art of the Near East. However, the artist had to take into account the *communicative* effectiveness of the symbols and that this latter had to be immersed in the truly plastic, without incurring in simplistic graphic-literary «Explanation» (see 22).

20. *Last version of the fallen horse.* White paper, graphite and crayons —large yellow background, plus other magenta stains and others in vermilion and blue, 0,24 × 0,45—. Autographed in French: *10th May 37 (IV).* The type of equine bestiality Picasso was after is totally achieved here by the surprisingly brutal deformations with which the head is given vigorous body, even despite its human jaw, and the lack of aggressivity in its weary gesture. (See 2, 3, 5, 6, 10, 13, 15, 17.)

21. *Second version of the mother with the dead child on the ladder:* White paper, graphite and crayons —yellow, magenta, vermilion and blue— 0,455 × 0,243. Autographed in French: *10th May 37 (V).* It is done in an impulsive style and powerful

colour which accentuates its pathetic expressionism. (See 16.)

22. *The god-like androcephalous bull:* White paper, graphite, 0,24 × 0,453. Autographed in French: *11th May 37.* (See 19.) (it cannot be called a «Minotaur» for it has a bull's body and not a man's). It may be, as is said, that the face is a reference to Dora Maar's, but above all, it shows the sum of intelligence and youth together with the all-powerful vigour of the drawing.

23. *First head of a suffering woman.* White paper, graphite and crayons —yellow, green, blue— 0,453 × 0,24. Autographed in French: *13th May 37 (I).* So far Picasso had not dealt with, had not *isolated* suffering on the female face. In this drawing, and in his own way, he carries out a detailed «anatomical» examination of the mouth, as the starting-point for all the deformations which will be necessary from now on to accentuate its expressivity. The iris of the right eye turns out to be the diaphragm of a camara, could this be a reference to his mistress, the photographer Dora Maar? (See 30-34, 38-42, 47-57, 59-61.)

24. *The hand of the warrior with the broken sword.* Paper, graphite, 0,24 × 0,45. Autographed in French: *13th May 37 (II).* In the photo of May 11th, the first we possess of **Guernica,** the hand had been solved, more or less in the same way as in the final work. In its tight, expressionist mass, six fingers can be counted. Many of the previous strokes are visible.

25. *The first of another series of different versions of the mother and dead child.* White paper, graphite and crayons —yellow, green and magenta, 0,24 × 0,45—. Autographed in French:

13th May 37 (III). The mother does not send her heart-rending sorrow upwards but over the child which sways in the air, barely held by its weak neck. Its dress becomes metamorphosed into two female breasts, whilst the woman's own are drawn ringed, somewhat phallic or in fish-like form. Both figures are dramatically shaken among highly dynamic compositional triangles. (See 36, 37, 52 and 58.)

26. *A reconstructive exploration of the bull's head*. Cloth-paper, graphite on grey and blue-grey wash, 0,23 × 0,29. Autographed in French: *20th May 37*. From the first photograph of the process of the work and after a great many attempts, the bull's head was practically solved fundamentally, which does not mean that Picasso did not feel the itch to change it or to reconstruct it, or, at least, to take it as a *marginal* task. In the present instance, it seems as if he had already dropped the idea that it could be human (see 19 and 22). However, certain humanoid features persist: the lips and chin, the thick cheeks and eyebrows in the form of two vegetable bouquets. The iris of the eyes is larger than the opening of the eye-lids. The same occurred with previous figures which he had drawn before. (See 23 and 25.)

27. *Second reconstructive exploration of the bull's head and further inventions for the eyes*. Cloth-paper, graphite on grey-white wash, 0,23 × 0,29. Autographed in French: *20thMay 37*. Now in a similar position to that it was to have in the fourth stage revealed by Dora Maar's photos (cf.). It has a sharp, cone-shaped tongue and horrified eyes. One of its nostrils looks like a small horn. A third eye is in one of its ears —see the previous

10. Mai. 37. (III)

bull's head—. Like the following one, which is carried out on a linealist basis, except that it has deliberate, very dark stains on the lower jaw and throat. In view of the vertical position of the paper, the skull seems short in relation to the rest.

28. *Penultimate version-sketch for the horse's head.* Cloth paper, graphite on greyish —white— wash, 0,29 × 0,23. Autographed in French: *20th May 37.* Now in a similar position to the final one at the fourth stage as shown in Dora Maar's photographs (see). Whith a pointed conical tongue and terrified eyes. One of the nostrils resembles a small horn. There is a third eye in one of the ears—see the head of the previous bull—like the following one, done in realistic style, except that it has intentional dark spots on Jaw and throat on account of the vertical placing of the paper, the skull seems short when compared to the following sketch.

29. *Last sketch version of the horse's head.* Cloth paper, graphite on grey wash, 0,23 × 0,29. The eyes look like propellors with the iris larger than the opening of the eyelid. There is another eye in each ear. See the two previous drawings.

30. *Second head of a suffering woman.* Cloth paper, graphite on grey wash, 0,30 × 0,23. Autographed in French: *20th May 37.* Linealist. Completely upturned and horizontal. The mouth is similar to the first, but has a sharp, coneshaped tongue. There is a sort of M in the form of a pair of gigantic eyebrows which may also be formed by two capital A's, and, if we insist on finding a monogram in it, and R: that is, Maar Dora. (See 34 and 36.) The face is still without tears.

31. *Third head of a suffering woman.* Cloth

paper, graphite on grey wash and creamy-white on the horse and some of the strokes of the mouth, 0,29 × 0,23. Autographed in French: *24th May 37*. Also linealist. Likewise with a sharp pointed tongue, but slightly curved and with an indication of natural roughness, attention being paid to its biological nature. Towards the top, its profile is drawn diagonally. The tears of blood appear. There is a blush scribbled on her cheek.

32. *Fourth head of a suffering woman.* Cloth paper, graphite on grey wash, 0,29 × 0,23. Autographed in French: *24th May 37*. The tongue is even more curved and biological than the former one. The profile is in vertical position. The tears are more curvedly drawn from the corresponding tear-ducts. Highly expressionistic.

33. *Horizontal male (?) head.* Cloth paper, graphite on grey-white and grey wash, 0,23 × 0,29. Autographed in French: *24th May 37*. This must have been a sketch for the dead warrior (see 44) although it is female. It would not be out of the way to relate this too with the female figure lying on the ground which was to disappear from the work (see the photographs of the process). The profile is turned upwards and is drawn over another done before this one with less pressure from the pencil and covered with gouache wash. The irises of the eyes are to be seen beneath the edge of the lower eyelid. The final work may be seen through the over-painting, next to a full view of a mouth.

34. *Fifth head of a suffering woman.* Cloth paper, graphite on grey wash, 0,23 × 0,29. Autographed in French: *27th May 37*. The profile is turned downwards to the right. The eyebrows form

20 *Last version of the fallen horse*

an M (see the easily guessed monogram of 30 which with slight variations, one can manage to decipher too in the brows of the mother with the dead child in flames, as well as in the male statue's palm in **Guernica**). The tears are curved and fall both up and down. The hair is violently streaked and darkened.

35. *Bearded man with arms raised*. Cloth paper, graphite on grey wash, 0,23 × 0,29. Autographed in French: *27th May 37*. The man is in a similar position to the flaming woman which already figured with raised arms in the first photo of the work's process dated 11th May, and which would take some time to acquire is final form.

36. *Second differentiated version of the mother with the dead child*. (See 25.) Cloth paper, graphite and crayons —vermillion, magenta and blue— on blue-grey wash and black ink with a brush, below, 0,23 × 0,29. Autographed in French: *28th May 37*. The child hangs from the front of its mother. Her breasts are in the form of artificial Freudian

144

dummies which are also to be seen on one of the women in **Guernica.** The tongue is sharp and cone-shaped. The tears are long and bloody. Between the eyebrows, although not so clear as in No. 30, one can guess the monogram mentioned above. (See 30 and 34.)

37. *Third differentiated version of the mother with the dead child.* Cloth paper, graphite, crayons —blue, green, magenta, vermilion, yellow— on grey wash with natural hair on the hair of the drawing. Was this a love fetish of Picasso's? 0,23 × 0,29. Autographed in French: *28th May 37.* Dark background with house, one of which is in flames. The child and one of the mother's hands are pierced by a broken lance —or thick arrow— and by a barely visible sabre from below, which at first glance is not noticeable. The woman is on the right, her face in horizontal position turned up-wards. One breast is frontwards —with two con-centric circumferences in another oval form; the

The god-like androcephalous bull **22**

The hand of the warrior with the broken sword **24**

other breast, ringed and with a *Freudian* dummy-nipple (see 36). In the bottom right-hand corner there is a strong whirlwind— a bomb?

38. *Sixth head of a suffering woman.* Cloth paper, graphite and crayons —yellow, blue, vermilion and magenta— on a light greyish-white wash, 0,23 × 0,29. Autographed in French: *28th May 37*. The profile looks upwards and is turned to the left. It is in front of a house with a window. The tongue is in the shape of an eye-tooth and there is supposedly —this time totally confused— the monogram of 30, 34 and 36 in the brows. The hair is standing on end in horror.

39. *Seventh head of a suffering woman.* Cloth paper, graphite and crayons —yellow, blue, magenta and vermilion— on a blue-grey wash 0,23 × 0,29. Autographed in French: *31st May 37*. This and the following ones up to number 42 inc. closely resemble one another: the head has no hair but something like ringed leeches on the nape of the

neck and is toothless. The tongue is sharp and cone-shaped, the eyes like popping curved carrots. This drawing has been reinforced over another of which five fingers of one hand and a house in flames can still be seen.

40. *Eighth head of a suffering woman*. Cloth paper, graphite and crayons —magenta, vermilion, yellow and blue— on a gray wash, 0,23 × 0,29. Autographed in French: *3rd June 37*. The eyebrows are now clearly reinforced in the shape of ears of wheat which could be just glimpsed in the previous drawing. Falling tears of blood have been added.

41. *Ninth head of a suffering woman*. Cloth paper, graphite and crayons —blue, yellow, green, magenta and vermilion— on a greenish-grey wash with other tints, 0,23 × 0,29. Autographed in French: *3rd June 37*. The eyelashes are in the form of vegetable bouquets.

42. *Tenth head of a suffering woman*. Cloth paper, graphite and crayons —blue, magenta, vermilion, yellow and green— on a grey wash, 0,23 × 0,30. Autographed in French: *3rd June 37*. The course of the tears is curved; the eyebrows are like the curved points of arrows and the «leeches» on the nape of the neck lose their orderly parallelism. (See 39.)

43. *The warrior's head between two (?) horse's hooves*. Cloth paper, graphite on blue-grey wash, 0,23 × 0,29. Autographed in French: *3rd June 37*. The head was drawn face downwards until the sixth photo taken by Dora Maar, although with very different characteristics to this one. Could Picasso still have been thinking of the position of this head only one day from the installation of the

work in the Spanish pavillion. (See the following.)

44. *The head of the warrior-statue*. Cloth paper, graphite on greyish-white and grey-blue wash, 0,23 × 0,29. Autographed in French: *4th June 37*. Was it drawn after the final head of the large canvas? Except that the large work could have been transported with great care on its frame and without having been rolled up. It may even have been taken in a special vehicle and it is not feasible that on the same day, the 4th June, the head should have been repainted. It is, however true, that one can make another conjecture. Did Picasso carry on painting **Guernica** between the 4th June, the date on which it was transported to the Spanish pavillion and the 12th June, when the exhibition was inaugurated? (See the previous number). There has certainly been a likeness pointed out between this head and that of a portrait of a Mozarabic saint lying down.

45. *The warrior's open hand*. Cloth paper, graphite on blue-gray wash, 0,23 × 0,29 Autographed in French: *4th June 37*. This poses the same problem as the previous drawings. The three could be the germinal idea for the works to follow, certainly *not* «preparatory» ones but done after **Guernica,** all of them having been carried out when the large work was transported to the Spanish pavillion in the Paris Exhibition (see above). Photographed by Dora Maar, it differs more than may be apparent at first sight from the one already portrayed. Perhaps it was to figure thus in **Guernica** from the fifth stage and is maybe only an example of Picasso's habit of re-working a theme which had already been solved.

27   *Second reconstructive exploration of the bull's head and further inventions for the eyes*

Works «a posteriori» of the assumed termination of «Guernica»

47. *11th head of a suffering woman*. Cloth paper, graphite on grey wash, 0,29 × 0,23. Autographed in French: *8th June 37*. See the two former ones. Linear drawing, with great decisiveness in the clean strokes. The profile is vertical and turned to the left. The tongue is fleshy and natural.

48. *12th head of a suffering woman*. Cloth paper, graphite and crayons —blue, green, magenta, vermilion, yellow— with gouache or oil-paint above the hair, 0,29 × 0,23. Similar to the

The sketch version of the horse's head **29**

previous one, but with contrasts of tone on account of the patches of colour used here. (See 47.)

49. *13th head of a suffering woman.* Cloth paper, graphite and crayons —green, blue, magenta, burned vermilion— on grey wash, 0,30 × 0,23. Autographed in French: *13th June 37.* Five days after the former one, Picasso went back to his «a posteriori» works on **Guernica,** taking the former head once more to deal with it in another way, although somewhat similar to the previous one. (See 47.)

50. *14th head of a suffering woman.* Cardboard stamped with a layer of greyish-white oil-paint,

graphite with touches of reddish, yellow, greenish and blue colours, 0,115 × 0,087. Autographed in French on the back: *19th June 37*. The face is practically horizontal. The sharp cone-shaped tongue returns (see 7). There is a barred (?) window to the left. A sort of A can be seen in the brows, turned into a long spider. (See 20.)

51.   *15th head of a suffering woman*. Canvas, oil-paint, 0,55 × 0,465. Autographed in French: *22nd June 37*. The woman dries her tears with a handkerchief, but on the opposite side to that on which the eyes are painted. These latter are of a similar shape to those in previous drawings, and are drawn in coloured pencils —yellow, green, blue, magenta and vermilion—. (See 54 and 55.)

52.   *Fourth differentiated version of the mother and dead child*. Canvas, oil-paint and graphite, 0,55 × 0,46. There is a data which is today partially visible: *22nd June 37* (?). Line-drawing. The head of the child is under the mother's chin next to her throat. She has a sharp, cone-shaped tongue, slightly curved. Her face has a window at the back of it.

53.   *16th head of a suffering woman*. Canvas, oil-paint, graphite and crayons —magenta and vermilion—, 0,55 × 0,46. Partially visible date: *26th June 37*(?). Similar to numbers 47-49. With notable rectifications of a certain formal importance.

17th head of a suffering woman. Canvas, oil-paint, 0,55 × 0,46. Dateless. The woman dries her tears with a handkerchief. Similar to 51, and apparently *never donated by Picasso to the New York* MOMA, therefore not received by the Prado.

54.   *18th head of a suffering woman*. Etching on paper, first stage, number 6 of an edition of 15

prints, 0,69 × 0,495. Signed in pencil: *Picasso*. Dated 2nd July 1937, together with the following one and numbers 59 and 60, of monstrously surrealist tuberosities. The woman dries her tears with a handkerchief. (See 51.)

55. *19th head of a suffering woman*. The second stage of the previous etching done in acquatint, number 4 of a series of 15 prints of equal dimensions and signature. The acquatint has been left out of the forehead, so that one can see a female behind in same and the corresponding female organ touched by one of the eyes in the form of the male gland. The hair, face, handkerchief and hands are intensely streaked.

56. *20th head of a suffering woman*. White paper, black ink in several densities and pen, 0,253 × 0,171. Autographed in French: *July 37*. The woman bites the handkerchief with which she dries her eyes. It is very carefully drawn, with special attention paid to volumetrics. The eyes still have the form of male glands.

57. *21st head of a suffering woman*. Brown-coloured paper, black ink and pen, 0,15 × 0,115. Autographed in French: *6th July 37:* Quite similar to the previous drawing but done in a more carefree and rapid style and infinitely less detailed.

58. *Fifth differentiated version of the mother and dead child*. Canvas, monochrome oil-paint —grey, white and black print—, 1,30 × 1,95. Dateless and without a signature. 26th September 1937. The mother holds the head of the child whose body floats in the air. There is a Freudian dummy-nipple on one of the mother's breasts. She is crying out with a curved, pointed tongue, and is kneeling on the ground. The artist has not bothered to cover

up the corrections and try-outs done on the child's head.

59. *22nd head of a suffering woman*. Brown paper, graphite, black ink and pen, 0,90 × 0,50. Autographed in French: *12th October 37*. There are certain bulbous likenesses to the following work and nos. 54-55. The woman has her fleshy tongue out. The neck is in the form of the base of a jug or sculptorial bust. The eyeballs seem to be surrounded by eyelids like small boats.

60. *23rd head of a suffering woman*. Canvas, oil-paint, charcoal, black ink and pen, 0,55 × 0,46. Dateless. 13th october 1937. See the former one. The woman dries her tears with a handkerchief (see 50). She still has similar boat-shaped eyelids and the eyeballs take on a larger aspect than before.

61. *24th head of a suffering woman*. Canvas, oil-paint, 0,92 × 0,73. Dateless, although thought to be the 17th. October, 1937. Green face and hands, blue handkerchief, magenta scarf, brown and black dress. There is little more than the shoulders, a scarf over her head, the woman biting and wringing the handkerchief in both hands.

The photographs of the seven stages and a fragment of the process of «Guernica»

As has already been said on several occasions, they were photographed by Dora Maar and published for the first time in «Cahiers d'Art». The work must doubtless have passed through other different stages, but we are lucky enough to be able to count on the following.

First stage: Charcoal drawing. Dated 11th May 1937. It would not be foolhardy to assume that before reaching this stage Picasso must have carried out, rubbed out and re-done a good deal more than we are shown in the photo as having been rectified. At the top of the picture, to the left, these changes are to be seen to best advantage: there is still part of a bull's head, front-on.

By means of large vertical lines and oblique angles, the geometrical structuring of the composition is thought out and planned. From left to right one can see: in its place just as —in the rest— it will be in the final work, the *mother and dead child.* The *bull's head,* profile to the left above a tormented woman who was in the work at first, the bull's body reaching the central zone of the work with its long tail. In the centre, there is *the horse,* which falls defeated, its neck curved, its head horizontal and its lower jaw upwards. The whole of its body forming an unmistakable dynamic oval which was to be the nucleus of the general elliptical compositional one indicated in the first «preparatory» drawing (cf.). The horse and a *naked warrior* are looking at each other. This latter is lying on the ground from more than half-way across the canvas to the left-hand side where his legs are drawn. His arm holds a broken sword and a flower springs from the hand, practically as they were to be painted in the final canvas, for the rest was to be *destroyed,* together with his other arm with its fist clenched (see «preparatory» drawing number 15). The *woman with the lamp* the building from which she leans out are both basically irremovable. Beneath them, *another woman* was to have the lower part of her body

33   *Horizontal male (?) head*

changed, at this stage taken up by a battered old chair. Beneath the previous woman there is a beautiful young woman lying dead, her breast bared. She possesses a feminine appeal that was to disappear after Picasso had also tried out the corpse of a man. Lastly, under the fire which comes out of the windows of the house in the background, there is the *woman in flames* who floats above ground-level impelled by her pain and whose left foot was to pass over to her left knee. As the saying goes, everything must be done at its due time and Picasso as yet does not even consider the toning or the effects of light and shade. He only draws a few forms and concepts which are *in his mind*. The rest was to come at the painting stage. The composition is most energetically and reflexively structured, but it still seems far too accumulative. Not even the flames make specific reference to the raid on the town of Guernica. There is no doubt that from the first Picasso wished to transcend this dramatic event to an even higher plane of emotion and thought, in such a way that his work would be in fact an allusion to all the monstrosities of all men, without distinction of race, ideology or flags.

Second stage: Picasso has already painted no small part of his work, but on the whole this is what he was to *destroy,* doubtless because he was to become eager to attack those parts of it which were precisely the ones which gave him most

Fifth head of a suffering woman   **34**

trouble and which were not to convince him completely: the neck and head of the horse —it has taken on the sharp, cone-shaped tongue— (see «preparatory» drawing no. 7) the head and chest of the warrior, the lower, longitudinal half of same, the beautiful young dead woman. The left foot of the woman in flames has now become part of the knees. A large flaming sun has been painted behind the raised fist, which now holds a sheaf of corn, although Picasso must already have decided to transform this or to eliminate the corresponding arm which has almost totally been covered over. Certain dark patches now begin to lend dramatic power to the composition drawn.

(Fragment of a stage of the ensemble which was not photographed.) Juan Larrea reproduced and commented upon it. With a few apparently simple changes and, indeed ingenious ones, the horse's head has not the lower jaw turned upwards. Next to its jaws a small anthropomorphic head of some small creature with a long straight neck appears and was to be wholly painted in the next stage. This was most likely on account of the inefficiency attained by simplistic symbols. On account of the placing of the ears and other forms around it, the horse seems to be crowned with an imaginable mitre (see this feature repeated several times in the *Dream and Lie of Franco*).

Third stage: The dark planes take on greater force and pathetic pictorial support. The dead warrior now turns his head to the left, although face-downwards. The horse's head is the same as in the previous fragment. The mother with the dead child has been surrounded by a uniform darkness. A hand with pointed fingers springs from between the breasts of the woman with the lamp. The woman below her has been endowed with morbidly female buttocks which reach as far as the edge of the painting and which were to be the main object with which the sensuality limited to this figure in the highly ascetic **Guernica** was to be underlined at first glance. The sun and raised fist have been drastically cut out. In their place an almond-shaped form appears which was to become a light-bulb in the seventh stage. To the left, near to the profile of the bull's head, something like a half-moon has been drawn. Picasso keeps to the extremely difficult golden rule of artistic creation: that which runs the greatest risk of not being valid: «he who takes on too much will hold on to little», that if a work is good, it is even better if it is brief. Picasso was not lacking in boldness when it came to sacrifice ideas and work, without any demurring whatsoever. There is no doubt that he sweated blood over his work and was ready to drastically change it whenever it did not come up to the elevated and profound creative goals he had marked for himself.

Fourth stage: The unhistorical *nocturnal character* of the work was now to be decided and arranged, thus dramatizing the scene. The neighing horse's head has been raised and is almost in its final stage. The body and hind-quarters of the bull take up the left side of the canvas and are so placed as to heighten its genitality next to the naked breasts of the woman with the dead child. The artist has worked a lot on the woman floating in flames, although she is still very much an amorphous heap of blotches. What was to be the head of a beautiful dead woman has been modified for the

35   *Bearded man with arms raised*

second time. The flower near her and the broken sword has disappeared. It seems that the scarf of the woman kneeling on the ground is made of *real* cloth, as the cloth which hangs from her waist is in fact, thus hiding one of her breasts. The other breast, has a *Freudian* dummy-nipple (see the second stage and «preparatory» drawing no. 7). The almond-shaped screen irradiates light, although the light-bulb was to be missing for quite a while yet. In the space between the neighing horse's mouth and the powerful neck of the bull, there is a white patch which in the following stage was perhaps to help us see more clearly that this is a cut made in a tree-trunk and had it been kept in

the final work, would have been the sole «Basque» reference in the work: that of the mythical tree of the bombed town of Guernica. Had someone annoyed him by insisting that the work was to have little or nothing *to do* with the catastrophic historical event chosen as «motif»? Did the temptation to bring in some «*descriptive*» symbol teem in his mind?

Fifth stage: The woman in flames is practically solved. The four sharp tongues of fire appear above the house behind her. The hand and left arm of the dead warrior are portrayed in the same place in which there had been a leg with its corresponding foot. The bull's genitals are drawn

39 *7th head of a suffering woman*

both simply and precisely. The dead woman lying on the ground disappears. The broken blade of the sword changes direction, now diagonally upwards. The woman with the lamp's house is given a roof and dark patches are inserted between the breasts and hand. The light-bulb is still missing. Although the work does not lose any of its dramatism, it certainly gains in the serenity of its dynamic ensemble.

Sixth stage: Real cloths are again hung from the canvas: from the mother with the dead child, the woman with the scarf and the one who floats in flames —in this latter what covers her body may be a piece of cardboard on which parallel stripes have been painted——. The light-bulb is still missing. The chopped-down tree (?) is still there. There are still the tears which appeared in the fourth stage on the woman with the scarf. An equivocal jumble of forms are still to be solved on the dead warrior, which, although interesting in themselves, are not so with regard to the function they perform in the work as a whole.

Seventh stage: A little more and the work could be called finished. The warrior's head has been turned upwards, thus lending it courage and formal imagination. Its body has been lost like a broken bust, the arm far from the broken sword on the hilt of which the flower has been painted.

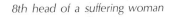

8th head of a suffering woman **40**

which was to disappear in the third stage. Between the horse's hind legs now with one of them dotted which reminds one of the «collages» done with printed letters —an arrow is drawn in— or is pointing towards the bull and the mother with the dead child, this latter now with little hanging feet. Behind and above the three —the bull, the mother and child— a corner of an interior is painted. The three (?) is replaced by a table on which a small bird is painted (settling or in the air?), which has an almond shape to the front and could well suggest the propellor of a plane spinning. Its neck is stretched up and is unfinished, its form being effectively that of a bird. The women's skirts at both sides are very simply decorated with parallel stripes. The foot in the lower right-hand corner has also taken on its final form. At last, the floor has been paved. The tears of the woman in the scarf are no longer needed. The houses to the right are almost totally finished.

Each and every one of the stages briefly mentioned here shows that **Guernica** implied a highly conscious intellectual act with none of the improvising capacity which nobody can deny Picasso. As work progressed, he sacrificed and modified whatever was necessary, despite the fact that this would have attained a highly precise pictorial and formal maturity. He drastically remodelled the baroque nature of the original accumulative design in search of ever arduous clarity and synthesis. It is quite clear that this came about through a type of expressionism that was as Spanish and Baroque as it was Picasso's own and derived from the nineteenth century.

«Guernica»

(Canvas, oil-paint, 3,50 × 7,80. Begun at the beginning of May 1937 and finished the 3rd or 4th of June of the same year.)

Its climaxes and symbolic characters

There has been a great deal written and said about these, although Picasso was to energetically avoid clarifying them verbally and nobody who has read up to here could really deny how he arranged or wished to arrange them. There is nothing in his great work which refers directly and explicitly to the circumstantial and spine-chilling event of the bombing raid on the town of Guernica, which occurred on the evening of the 26th April 1937. It was carried out to its destructive end by German planes and pilots in the service of the anti-Republican uprising of General Franco. Neither is there any reference to this latter, to his minions or emblems or to the Republic which he attacked, although this historical work was painted at the commission and in favour of the cause of this latter. Everything in the work was to be *metaphorically transcended to an even higher intellectual and moral plane,* that of ideas, repulsion and feelings. The international press was to throw the first stone at the bellicose brutality of Guernica and the outcry which followed for the massacre carried out on a rearguard in which there could only have been, old people, women and children, for all the other «useful» men were fighting on the front. Not long after this, the verb «to conventrize» was to be invented, London and Berlin were to be massacred, Hiroshima and Nagasaki razed to the ground and there was to be no respite until finally today, we possessed the «defensive» neutron bomb. As annihilating for humans alone, we should judge it as «bestial», against our nature. Thus, **Guernica** had

43   *The warrior's head between two (?) horse's hooves*

be a historical work, but not in the same way as others had been in the past. Not even in the same way such distinguished creations as Velázquez's *Lanzas* or the *3rd of May Executions* by Goya were to be. For Picasso, the dimension through which the universal could be contemplated or intued was quite different in the middle of the 20th century, so that his work could no longer be the simple narration of events. It had to express itself in the way in which only symbolic reconfigurations can.

There was perhaps only one precedent of this in the past and that was in the symbolism of the «emphatic caprices» with which Goya finished off his also historical *Disasters of war*. In this way, in the form of nine *universal and generalizing symbols,* all the others which Picasso was obliged to compose and portray were to operate in *Guernica*. These were the ancient mythical, conceptuated *animal symbols:* the easily terrified but even so, *fecund female figure; infanticide,* the most horrifying of crimes; the an-

The head of the warrior-statue **44**

tagonistic *lamps* which can blind so many to so much —blur the vision— as likewise provide clarity of vision; the *darkness of night;* domestic *interiors,* which though homely and endearing, are brutally invaded by violence; the *iconoclastic* destruction of the ideal transmuted into the male statue; *ars* manufactured to be broken; and the *poetical* flower which is born and re-born among the corpses. (It should be noted that in **Guernica** there is no *strictly* dead man, perhaps because these latter are the ones who kill or who are obliged to kill.) From left to right, the following symbols correspond to the generic one of femininity: *maternity worse than assassinated* —with the dead child next to her skirt-womb; that of *Eros vanquished*— the pregnant (?) woman kneeling on the ground with her Freudian dummy-nipples (see stages 2 and 3 and drawing no. 7 of the «preparatory» series) her morbid buttocks and sexual vulva on show to all eyes, albeit small and in the shade; that of the *humble light,* which is hardly a technical means of illumination, being ancient, popular and rustic in quality, although even thus it manages to throw its unsuspected moral splendor; the *pathetic woman in flames,* although nobody should take the materiality of her floating body to be spiritual. The generic symbol of infanticide can only be represented by itself, and can only belong to itself, for with it, all that is clean in the world, *innocence,* is killed. To the counterposed lamps correspond the symbols of their disparity: there is the *humanized light,* primitive and homely, under control in the intimacy of family life, that of the lamp, and that of the *highly technological light* which does not seem much, but which however should be carefully considered. Nobody can guess how far it is to go in its technical reality. This is the light from the light-bulb which shines over all. The generalizing, universal symbol of the male statue contains that of *destructivity*, which innate human aggressiveness must put an end to —however useless this may be— when the human race is reborn with a lucid will of permanence (see the chapter on the *Minotauromachy* engraving). Thus, as far as it refers to conceptuated animality, the fact that *equivocal myths* also exist concerns this symbol: such as that of the horse which, demythified, could well turn out to be a destroyer; or that of the bull, which is both powerful and awesome, but in whose elemental force —in the fecund and even religious energy it has represented from time immemorial—, one might find a hope, however frightening its appearance may be. (Thus so far, without daring to enter upon conjectures as to the highly confusing *dove-chick-plane* or the very simple *table*.)

Larrea played with the words «madre» (mother)=«Madrid», when referring to the dead child, for in 1937 Madrid was defending itself tooth and nail against the tough seige of General Franco. But he could also have added another noun, thus developing the verbal symbolic concatenation: «madre-matriz-Madrid»: «mother-matrix-Madrid». It should also be remembered that, although we prefer to know a painter's symbols through his pictorial configurations, Picasso enjoyed writing out the streams of surrealist automatisms of the mind and their language. According to him, each must see in the picture what he wants to see. Thus, for example, the whole of the foregoing interpretation in the sense that the bull could be none other than the intrahistorical *Iberian* bull. He is so much one of this species that —whether he is roaring through his mouth with its obus-tongue— nobody and nothing could touch or wound him, thus representing the only unhurt reality in the composition. The horse is indeed a horse, but he has been pierced and mortally wounded, falling to the ground like the statue which he has brutally kicked and the body of which he has caused to disappear almost entirely, in annihilating unison —for wars rarely give victors and vanquished. He was a horse of *pseudo-printed* paper; the word «death» rhetorically part of popular speech, a long rigmarole in sham moulded bodies, despite his tremendous neigh and the enormous *obus* —or unheard-of tongue made with a steely, hurtful gland— which he appears to shoot from his jaws. The broken statue on the ground, dead or in its last throes of agony, is the ill-treated and dismembered image of another ideal among the conceptions of existence which make men kill and kill each other, thus reaching the most hidden nook and cranny of the home, eclipsing, darkening the short day of our lives. It is true that when painted a bull is a bull, and a horse is a horse, just as Picasso, in a moment of bad temper, stated. But they can be painted for very different reasons and with very different meanings: for the mere pleasure of painting them, as participants in a landscape, a story or anecdote; or, following an atavistic transmuting symbolist mechanism, in order to pour into them concepts, virtues —«forces», whether benign or otherwise— which only concern man's satanic or «divine» facets, but never merely themselves. Like-

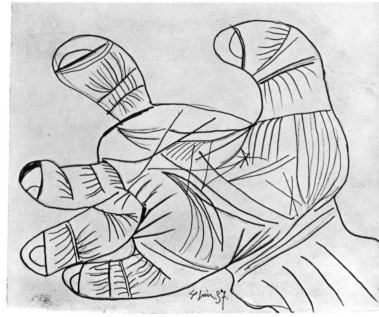

The warrior's open hand **45**

wise a lamp is a lamp, but when it is brandished
with such majestic force and by such a «classical»
Picassan woman, it must lead us to think that it
represents the small, intimate light of those who,
whilst they do not possess other blinding lum-
inaries, bear the splendour of the authentic and
vital even in their faces. For the impetus of the
woman with this simple, domestic light, is vital and
spendidly authentic. Thus, too, the flower is a
flower and, nevertheless, from the beginning of the
work, it had been portrayed as born from a broken
hand and sword, next to the beauty of a young
dead woman who, in the end, was to disappear in
order to eliminate all facile sentimentalism. It is

also true that this flower was once plucked, but it grew again. For the *creative, poetic* hand of the flower had to be juxtaposed as a sign, if not of hope, then at least of the spirit which is ever threatened but ever reborn.

In the same way, the light-bulb is a light-bulb. But, for those who have lost the fertile capacity of amazement, for those who, like Picasso, know how to go through life with their faces marvelling at it, and who, like him would make a bull's head out of the seat and handle-bars of a bicycle thrown on a rubbish-heap, the light-bulb must represent a technical prodigy before which they must bow in awe, stupified day after day, however familiar we have become with them. For they know that it is a portent of human technique, one of a long series conquered, some of which were not so fortunate. It is both a technological and a verbal symbol, for what is in the lamp is no more nor *less* than a *bomb* («bombilla» in Spanish) under the not in-nocent light of which beasts and humans suffer. From the technology of the simple light-bulb, man has ridden frenetically on in search of technologi-cal shrapnel bombs, incendiary bombs, nuclear bombs, hydrogen bombs, neutron bombs... plus the contraptions with which to make them kill *from above*. This is a fact that everybody knows and that nobody could not think about. Clair-voyance is one of the genial painter's gifts and as an artist can and should prophesy. That among artists, few have done this seriously means little. At least before Picasso, Goya did it more than once. Who, if not him, in the *Black paintings,* after so much Phydian beauty, Raphaelite loveliness, superhuman Michael Angelisms and Roccoco hed-

onism, could reveal the tenebrous pus of multitudinarian, massified humanity?

More than a century ago, Goya wrote that «the
dream of reason produces monsters». He would
also have written that «the dream of technology
wakes not even with hecatombs». Let it be under-
stood that Goya would have written this without
any maudlin defeatism, perhaps flying at super-
sonic speed from Madrid to New York and perhaps
wishing to travel even to the moon. In the same
way, Picasso did not paint defeated either. For he
well knew that the proceating, primary and elemental bull fostered a hope for the strong and
natural. This should be said without forgetting that
Picasso himself said that «those who try to explain
paintings are usually totally wrong». For he was
also quite right when he stated that «I should like
to arrive at a stage where the way I have painted a
work could never be seen. What can this matter?
What I want is that my works should produce
emotion and no more than emotion». The trouble
is that on paintings and art in general, people are
convinced that it is even advisable to leave
evidence of their own emotions and thoughts by
transmitting them to others, albeit in the knowledge that, even when they are good ones, their
explanations can interfere with and complicate the
spontaneous perception of the innocent spectator
to whom the explanations are addressed.

Painting and composition

Even among people with a certain artistic
training and taste for the avant-garde, there are

those who, not without a certain connaisseur's smile, will minimize **Guernica** and exclaim «What a great poster!» forgetting that, for a start off, the poster —as likewise drawings and paintings— is a pictorial genre in which it is also possible to display genius in the work and lend it universal resonance. It is true that **Guernica** is just this, a *poster,* an enormous advertisement of what happened and could continue to happen; a *placard* for the loud-voiced public of the gigantic mass media of today, and a *mural,* it does not matter that it is painted on canvas: a *witty reality* which could just as well be carried through the streets by many, and placed in any main square of any town or village.

Guernica is without doubt the most famous work of art of our century, the most noticed show-piece of the most relevant of twentieth-century painters, who, thirty years before he painted the tremendous canvas, invented Cubism with *Les Demoiselles d'Avignon,* and, when Cubism seem to have passed into history and become definitely surpassed, carried out this great *poster-mural-placard,* a colossal painting and even greater creation of the spirit, a work which could not have been the fruit of lucid plastic creative investigation of forms and their syntax alone, but of this and a great deal more: the formidably painted ethos of a whole drama worthy of universal consideration.

His flat paintings belong to the Cubism of **Guernica;** his formal simultaneism —the front-on eyes in faces in profile—, the horse's crotch or the buttocks of a woman with her face to the spec-tator which, on account of the positions of their respective bodies, should have been hidden from view...; the imbricated and interfering marquetry of the formally representative surfaces of plastic invention; the highly cerebral recreation of the visible; the full intellectualization of the drawing; the inorganic geometry, which organizes at the same time as it is convulsive and dismembering; space and perspective as mental things; the arduous, reflexive and monumentalizing syntax —one might almost say muralist—, Cubism of **Guernica** which, because it obeys the mechanisms of human intellective perception, is also enriched by the not useless incursions into the living and spontaneous world of children's drawings which Picasso had made at least from 1933 onwards. These experiences were submitted to the discipline of «adult» art but are none the less noticeable and functional. That is, this was so plus the intricate wisdom which surrealism had furnished to the artist's subconscious.

It has also been said that **Guernica** is «a great black and white drawing», hardly a painting, on account of the lack of colours and the apparent lack of taste for textures. It is true that it was painted in only black and white and grey, which is a mixture of the former two, the work flowing from these tones in such a self-assured way that one would have thought that it sprang *alla prima,* without the efforts revealed by the stages which have come down to us in the photographs, the lines and dripping brush-strokes not mattering. It has been done with the palette of distilled synthesis, the same with which, Velázquez and Goya were to attain exceptional chromatic effects although naturally with quite different purposes and results. It was painted with noble black which in the hands of Spanish painters has asserted itself as

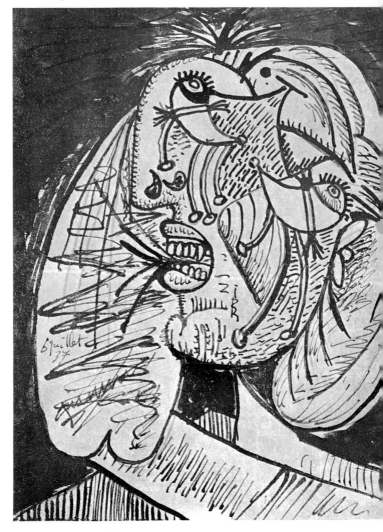

a colour and not as the absence of same. **Guernica** is painted with the highly severe emotional ascetism which evokes Zurbarán and because its subject did not by any means demand that it should be decked out in gay colours. There is nothing more consequent nor suitable than these *mere* whites, blacks and greys. Nothing could have permitted the force of the transcendent event and its characters, its whole metaphor to come over more directly to the spectator, who is thus left in disconcerted anguish. He thus smashes the rigid schemas handed on to him by an outdated education, mental laziness itself and the lack of taste for whatever is not already chewed over and digested or worse than digested.

If we so wish, we can draw in vertical compartments to the composition. This has been done with an accurate eye, for the numerous rules and measuring apparatus which Picasso the geometrician used, were handled in such a way that this could not be done with candid mathematical exactitude. Each of the compartments to be obtained thus will turn out to be valid in itself: they will be fragment-pictures of the totalizing compositional emotion; full entities in their own right, although parts of another fuller and greater one. In the first, the upwards movement of the semi-tensed arc is given by the head of the iconic male statue which is turned upwards, the head of the mother which is also turned upwards and whose lament mingles with the bull's roaring, the bull only looking at us, whilst the hanging head of the child seems like a dead, terrifyingly flaccid dart, the hand of the warrior statue awaiting its fall. In the second, widely-based compartment there is the horse's neigh which mingles with the luminous uproar of the light-bulb; there are also the horse's eyes dazzled by the light of the lamp which intimidates it; its pierced body and the arm broken by kicks with the sword from which a flower springs. Taken vertically, the third compartment suffices with two women, both with their faces turned towards something which does not matter and which we shall never see, the one below with the pathetic fall of her arms which flank her obvious femininity: breasts, belly and sex. The last compartment in this compositional series is perhaps the least attractive, but is highly success-ful and severly dramatic. This is an exact response to the mother at the other side, that is the woman with the frail body consumed by the flames, as though thrust out of the door to her right and who raises her arms in pain as high as the fire behind and above the house, either floating or about to fall onto a huge leg and foot.

Another compartmented, compositional reading of **Guernica** could be given by means of triangles which, in a similar way to the foregoing, and in view of Picasso's mutilating geometry, one should not expect to be elucidated with the simplis-tic sharpness of a straight drawing-pen. Neither should one expect them to be represented on the strength of pre-established point in the angles and other axes of the symmetry of the picture's strict format. To do thus would be to ignore the type of mathematics that Cubism meant and how **Guerni-ca** links its own structure with the expansive explosion of its planes, symbols, bodies, gestures and emotionally resonant expressions. Some of these deranged and deranging triangles are in full view —they are even underlined by the painter— and, all together, they are perhaps too numerous to annoy the reader,spectator of the work with a detailed discussion of each. Let him look at them for himself, if he so wishes, for this is probably an intellectual game which would maybe interest him as much as knowing that the horse's body is the displaced and displacing agitating nucleus of what is like an ellipse —by no means exactly regular— in which the statue-head, the mother, the bull's neck, the lamp, the head of the woman with the lamp, the line of the huge breast of the woman in flames, the morbid buttocks of the one below, the hand on the sword... all flow incessantly, round the same path and in an endless vibrating orbit.

Whatever other unrivalled compositions Picasso may have had in mind, and even within sight, when he carried out this intricate —Baroque— personal, ancient and modern, Cubist, work called Guernica, is anyone's guess. He knew a lot about everything which had been done and was being done, but he never forgot the aphorism that in art, plagiarism is that which is not followed by murder. If he indeed «laid his hands on» anything for his work, it is highly probable that it was not before his eyes and even that he did not even remotely remember it: that is, what he had already digested and re-digested was to spring from his fertile subconscious. This is said in the knowledge that the scholar must hesitate before speaking of «influences», for the *coincidences* are just as real or even more so. It is therefore very easy that gestures, postures and attitudes (precisely because their number is not infinite) may resemble each other or those of other works, and that, starting

184

from similar approaches and working towards goals which in some way converge, one can and often does arrive at similar conclusions. The same thing happens in art as in many other activities of man. Picasso is a *historicist* painter, having taken in copious and turbulent contributions from the past. Without any wish to underestimate him, quite the contrary in fact, the painter Pancho Cossío (1894-1970) called him the «Lafuente Ferrari of contemporary painting», thus relating him to the art historian Pancho most respected. Shouting his intentions to the four winds, Picasso would amuse himself by tackling *sui generis* versions of Cranach, Grünewald, El Greco, Velázquez, Murillo, David, Delacroix, Courbet or Manet. But **Guernica** is compositionally and artistically so individual that we must be extremely cautious when we look for alien or historical «antecedents» in it. The important ones are those which are to be found in Picasso himself, in his dense, overwhelming and multiform creative self.

INDEX OF ILLUSTRATIONS

* **Illustration in colour.**